Courage, dear heart

How to look back, learn and leap forward

Nic Crisp

DEDICATION

For my 2 gorgeous girls, Ella and Amy, may you
do it your way with strength, love, kindness
and confidence.

You cannot be truthful if you are not courageous.

You cannot be loving if you are not courageous.

You cannot be trusting if you are not courageous.

You cannot require into reality if you are not courageous.

Hence courage comes first and everything else follows.

- Osho. *Courage: The Joy of Living Dangerously*

CONTENTS

Preface

I am an Exec Coach. I have led, coached and worked alongside thousands of professional people, leaders, senior execs, MDs and Chief Execs over the past 25 years.

There is one question I always ask clients when I take them on: What would you do if you knew you couldn't fail?

It is generally the one they say they find the hardest. Not always because they don't know the answer, but to dare to write down in black and white dreams long held somehow makes it more real.

Over the years my clients have told me that if they knew they couldn't fail they would love to set up their own business, be a wedding planner, run a children's clothing company, write a book, be an MP, retrain as a lawyer, relax, take more risks and tell others what they really think. Some dream of a radical change of context, for others just a change in how they show up and importantly, how they spend their time. All reminding me that one can never, ever judge what we see on the outside.

Courage, dear heart

So this book shares some of their stories; how leaders who, just like me, having built successful careers and identities have ended up coming to a break point through crisis or calling and at that point have a choice to make: to follow their heart and their dream, or do what they think they should and play it safe.

The thoughtful, rich and searingly honest conversations I have had in 121 and group sessions over the years have amazed and inspired me. They have given me an insight into who people really are behind the mask we at times present and what is possible when we take the time to reflect and tune into the longing of the heart and the voice in our head that can prevent us from ever acting upon it. They have also taught me about myself: who I am and what I am here to do. Which, in a nutshell, is alignment.

Alignment between what we say and what we do which drives trust.

Alignment between what we stand for and how we show up, which is a marker of integrity.

Alignment between the head and the heart which drives both peace of mind and fiery purpose - a winning combination when it comes to unlocking the energy for results.

Alignment in who we are and what we share with the world, which brings joy; to us and everyone around us.

Alignment which is underpinned by the truth that, as leaders, whatever we ask of others must always start with the self.

As a trained facilitator I am also a great believer in the importance of sharing lived experience; of reviewing learning as a collective so that it may inspire, guide and create a template for how to get results, over and over again and fast. Story telling is an ancient practice; designed to pass on customs, beliefs and values over time, long before the written word was born. Story telling fosters learning, serves to inspire and creates a sense of belonging in individuals that we are connected and that we are not alone in experiencing the same challenges, dilemmas and triumphs. Listen to any 20 min TED talk and it is clear that the art of storytelling and sharing of the human experience is as relevant and powerful now as it ever has been.

Courage, dear heart

Over the past couple of years, I have been stepping out a little myself; letting my voice be heard a little wider, sharing my own experiences, reflections, insights and those of my clients on social media. I have watched the momentum, engagement and comments from friends of friends and complete strangers grow in line with my own confidence.

"*Why don't you write a book*" whispered my heart? (Not to mention a few friends of mine.)

"*Because you have no idea how, for a start*" said the voice of doubt in my mind.

But more than that was the fear of putting myself out there. Being a writer just happened to be one on my list of things I would do if I knew I couldn't fail. Which of course is a good enough reason to give it a go, given the subject matter.

So I am writing a book which charts the story of my work. I am writing it to share what I have learned along the way from my own experience. I also share the experiences of those I have coached over the years who willingly also shared their experiences, doubts, fears, dreams, failures and triumphs so that it might be a source of inspiration and practical help. I am writing for anyone wanting to find the courage to follow their heart. I am writing to practice what I preach as I start this next phase of my career.

So if you have been sitting with a dream that just won't go away and a list of reasons why you can't do it, then this book is for you... and maybe someone you know or lead who feels the same.

I want it to embody the simplicity and purpose I strive for across all areas of my work:

- Sharp insights that help you to see with fresh perspective.

- Simple tools and frameworks that work from lived experience not theory.

- Practical alongside support to help you make sense of wherever you are at, with honesty and creativity so that you can move forward with clarity, pace and purpose.

You will be the judge of that, and I look forward to hearing what you think.

Courage, dear heart

But for now, what would your answer be?

What would you do if you knew you couldn't fail?

Chapter 1: The wakeup call

"It's impossible," said pride.

"It's risky," said experience.

"It's pointless," said reason.

"Give it a try," whispered the heart

-   Anon

At the age of 40 I had what could classically be described as a mid-life crisis.

I desperately wanted to make the part of my job I loved most my main job.

I wanted to develop people.

I wanted to support leaders to get results fast as I had learnt how to do through training, practice and hard work.

I knew it was something I was gifted at, I knew that I had something that kept getting me promoted and made me a sought-after mentor and coach in the organisation and outside of it.

I now had a calling - a want to do more, be more. A longing and no idea how that was going to happen which for me at that time felt a scary place to be. For the best part of a year I struggled and fought the growing feeling of unease and disconnect. I had been asked to take the job that 10 years earlier had been my dream, I felt highly valued, I had a brilliant boss who afforded me much flexibility and opportunities, I was earning good money and I had a team I loved.

But I was unhappy. And unhappy with a propensity to tell myself that I shouldn't be: "*I mean what is wrong with you, what more do you want, you ungrateful cow*?"

My partner at the time was a consultant and coach. Through him I had been training outside of the organisation on my free weekends for about 5 years, taking part in and supporting programs created by Brad Brown and Roy Whitten (More to Life) that are in essence about making the unconscious drivers of our minds conscious. Just before my 40th Birthday in April my partner asked me to accompany him on a job in Paris with a team wanting to align and sharpen their strategy. It went well for us both. I valued the window into a world I wanted to step into and, surprisingly for him; he valued having some alongside support having worked for the best part of 10 years on his own. At the end of the weekend he floated the idea of me joining him in his business. It seemed like the perfect solution. I had a way out to do what I wanted, and I took it. I put the wheels in motion and by the August I was handing back my company car, saying goodbye to the friends, colleagues and teams I had worked alongside. I was full of hope and acknowledgement but not a huge amount of detailed planning for my new adventure. Two weeks later on the eve of our return from a family holiday to the USA and the dawn of my first project, my partner told me that he didn't want to be in the relationship anymore which spelled an ending both personally and professionally. For the first time since the age of 14 I found myself without a man or a job.

Not having either turned out to be the making of me. But that insight didn't come until a little later. First, I had to face straight into the pain. With 2 young children to support and a mortgage to pay I also had to start making a plan. And quick.

What I did in the following 12 months to create a successful business from a standing start will form the backbone of the story that follows. For now though, the first point to note about following your heart is that it always starts with a call to action: a calling or a wakeup call. Either will work, and if you are really lucky you might just have both.

Having 'a calling' can sound a rather dreamy affair; a heady mix of vision, hope, desire, passion, fiery purpose: something that is undeniably pulling you forward. Making it happen, 'the how', often requires other skill sets, behaviours, building blocks and tools. The 'how' is all about the practical, the doing; some of which may come naturally, some you may need support with. But the vision, a clear purpose and sharp attention to 'the how' are all equally important if you want great execution and results.

Something that applies to leading organisations and teams as much as it does our own lives and careers.

What I have learnt about having a calling is that sometimes it emerges as a vision, a question from the inside or from another that asks: "What if?" or "Have you ever thought about...?"

A thought you think you can put away in a box but that doesn't seem to want to go away.

Sometimes however it emerges as purposefulness from pain, because sometimes it really does take a crisis to create change.

In 'Our Iceberg is Melting' (Kotter, 2017) which is written as a fable, John Kotter outlines the issues real life organisations tend to run into in spotting the signs of change, the issues they encounter when they try to change and how to creatively solution to adapt quickly and overcome them. A looming crisis or a burning platform can create a sense of urgency and inspire creativity, but sometimes actual pain rather than a fear-based projection "if we don't do this (something we really don't want) will happen..." is what it takes. Sometimes organisations simply need to lose: whether that be financial targets, valued customers, market leadership or indeed their reputation, in order to shape up and be better. Sometimes the most brutal of wake-up calls are required to shake us from denial and get honest about how things really are.

One of my clients is Essex County Fire and Rescue. I started working with the Board and former Chief Fire Officer Adam Eckley back in Jan 2015. When I first spoke to Adam the organisation was in crisis. After a series of serious allegations of bullying and harassment, and a very tragic case that led to a fire fighter taking his own life, Adam invited in an independent external auditor, Irene Lucas, to review the Service Culture. He wanted an honest, unbiased assessment and to use it as a catalyst for change. The report was critical of Leadership practices, HR led process orientation, accepted behaviours and lack of transparent, 2 way open and honest dialogue. It also exposed a massive disconnect between how the Service was viewed internally vs. externally.

Amongst the general public on the outside they were rightly seen as highly valued and respected professionals who do an outstanding job in challenging circumstances, who put themselves at risk to protect and take care of the public, our homes and communities.

On the inside however, there was a belief that at times the team were not always taking care of each other and not speaking up. In essence, the organisation had a massive integrity issue that came at a huge personal cost to some employees, something that had shown up for years in Essex and in Fire Services up and down the country. But that report was the turning point. It brought the issues into the light, it galvanised energy to be better, and out of it came a clear vision, with values co-created by those in the organisation at all levels, a more open 2-way dialogue, changes to the leadership team to support greater alignment, and a pace and action for change.

Adam left the Service in April 2018 an infinitely better place than when he took over as Chief: financially, operationally and culturally. He is without doubt one of the most resilient, committed and inspiring leaders I have ever worked alongside. He is also one of the most humble, self-aware and open to support and personified another lesson we will come to: if you want to emerge like a phoenix from the flames of pain, then it helps to open up to the support, outside perspective and skills of others rather than attempt to figure it all out yourself. As Adam says 'you have to let go of the ego, the need to think you have to provide all the answers. You don't. And the more you engage, trust, and tap into the strengths of people around you, the quicker and easier you get to where you want to go".

I think he is absolutely right.

So sometimes the pain comes in the form of an event, or series of events that brings us into sharp alignment with reality - that all is not well; that something needs urgent attention and continuing to ignore, deny, or pretend it is in anyway different will no longer wash.

Any kind of loss or ending, like redundancy or being let go, that we did not see coming or want, are classic trigger events at an individual level. I have coached many people coming to terms with, and moving on from, the loss of a job, which when it happens to those in senior executive positions, tends to come swiftly. Almost always when I start the coaching, the conversation starts with "I don't know how this happened, one minute everything was fine, the next I'm being told that the Board have no confidence and they want me to go." However, by the end of the coaching engagement, the reflection is rarely regarded by the individual as true.

As one Director said to me: "Nic, I knew things weren't right. I thought that the answer was to do what I was doing, only more, faster, harder. But that only made it worse. I should have had an honest conversation. I should have challenged the Board and confronted the issues, but I didn't. In the end they came for me". He was compromised out, he found another very good job, but it took a great deal longer for him to truly grasp the importance of this insight. It took another repeat failure: this one with a sizeable emotional fall out before he truly got the lesson. As human beings we can get really good at avoiding: only seeing what we want to see, getting fixed on one solution; the ones we think we have control over when we feel least in control; of pretending, making up stories of how we want things to be. Whether we label it 'fantasy' or 'wishful thinking', our minds are powerful generators that can more than happily keep us safely stuck in denial and our own imaginary world. But when it comes to facing the truth, deep down we often know.

I would class my own situation as one of these examples. If I had been honest with myself then I knew that our relationship was not working and that I had not thought through the plan to join my then-partner's business. I was avoiding the reality of the details in order to escape a job I didn't want to be in anymore. But at that point I was still fixed on seeing things as I *wanted* them to be, not as they actually *were*. The signs were there: he wasn't clear, I wasn't happy, and neither were my girls, but the fear of repeating another pattern, of calling time on another relationship and a belief that I could not be on my own kept me hanging in. Which is another interesting thing about the crisis. The pain, when it comes, can welcome in with it a surprising amount of relief at not having to keep it all together. Once out in the open, and with the weight of pretence lifted, a space is created to consider other options. Even if you have no idea what to do next, the space creates freedom.

I did some research for a course I intended to write a year ago, the germ of an idea that eventually became this book. I first put an advert to friends, ex colleagues and connections on LinkedIn asking for people who had made big midlife career changes who would be willing to be interviewed. I also contacted people close to me who I knew had made big changes. I wanted to hear and learn from the experiences of others to identify where I could be of most support:

What had driven them to make the change?

What was the trigger?

What did they know now that they wish they had known before? Did they have any regrets?

What were their current challenges?

I talked to senior marketing, sales and HR professionals who had become consultants, teachers, lecturers and book keepers: accountants who had become coaches: many more who had started businesses in fields that bore absolutely no relation to their previous experience but were totally in line with their passions out of work. What I found with them, as I found with my clients, was that for many the trigger came from external loss and an internal sense of disconnect to something deeper. For some panic, physical pain. For others that flat feeling of boredom. Their stories highlight 3 common states:

The flatness of Obligation and Duty

- "I felt something was missing. I wanted something on a deeper level. I wanted to do something that mattered to me and use the skills I have with others but doing what I was doing, I just felt flat."

- "I felt unfulfilled, unsatisfied and disillusioned in my job. At the same time, I was fearful about how I would make it work; not being able to pay the mortgage. Then the company I was working for called me out that I was not engaged. I was forced into it in a way. I talked myself out of it a few times, because of the security; paying the bills. I was on a treadmill just doing the same thing over and over every day. Now I wished I had done it earlier. I wasn't happy; it was obvious, and they made the call in the end."

- "I felt frustrated and drained. I was in a business partnership that wasn't working – for either party. In many ways my confidence had grown but when it came to having honest conversations with my business partner I was procrastinating and reverting back to being 'too nice' rather than commercial. In the long run it doesn't do anyone any favours. I really disliked some of the childish behaviours I was developing as a result; focusing on the minutia and deflecting."

- "I had an extremely long commute and after 10 years driving 3-4 hours each day, I was starting to feel the strain: both mentally and physically with back ache. I felt as though most of my life was either spent at work or in transit. We'd invested a lot of time in creating a lovely home, we lived in a great little town and I was hardly ever there. I think I did a rough calculation in my head about the amount of time I had spent travelling over the past 12 months and it was crazy. My career was going well but I didn't feel particularly stretched in role and I wasn't enjoying it enough to justify the sacrifice."

A lack of fulfilment, boredom, disconnection; of being unchallenged can be one that creeps up over time. A feeling that we often override with a sense of duty, obligation to fulfil the practical sides of our lives: to make money, contribute to family income, pay for childcare, school fees, the family holiday - the endless list of stuff, some of which you may identify with. Whilst we know that the dull ache is there, the head rather than the heart is in the driving seat. This is akin to sleep-walking, getting up, getting dressed, doing the drive down the motorway and getting to work not really sure how you got there. Working through a routine in body not in spirit, time passes by and you are hardly there at the wheel to notice. But you know you are in a state of obligation if you feel the dull ache in your body and a mind that is in charge, telling you that you have to carry on. For most of the people in the camp of obligation, it was a wake-up call from someone else that shocked them into the present. They were moved on, a boss or loved on gave them some straight feedback or an ultimatum, someone close was no longer there and in one moment they were forced to face to reality of their situation and make a choice. They were forced to take responsibility which, when in obligation, is actually the one thing you are avoiding.

The Stress of Juggling

- "I went back to work after having had my second baby. Financially I was no better off and I felt as though I was doing neither job properly. And if I was going to leave my children in a nursery, I wanted to do something I actually enjoyed"

- "Everything was a bit manic, and I didn't feel I was giving my husband the time he deserved. During the week I would be getting home at 8pm, then going to bed at 9.30 to allow me to get up at 5.30am...getting on the 6.20am train into London. We lived for the week end and even then, I was still falling asleep half way through Strictly Come Dancing after just the one gin and tonic!"

- "I knew I was out of balance but most people I spoke to were shattered on a Friday and working longer and longer hours. I thought I could handle the relentless pressure and stress of my senior role. I was, and still have the propensity to be, addicted to the buzz of work. I am naturally competitive, driven/bossy and slightly over ambitious; this means I often bite off more than I can chew. I worked in a high performing team of people that I genuinely respected and I would do anything to ensure we won as a team. I wanted the business to be a great place to work and I worked tirelessly to achieve this vision. This meant early mornings, late nights and putting the job before almost everything else. "

- "There was a build-up of things over 2 – 3 years and I was not quite sure how to make it right. I had my baby, was traveling a lot, I couldn't spend the time I wanted with my baby, I hated the red tape and corporate rubbish of the company I was in. So I resigned - much to everyone's shock, including my own!"

- "I was suffering from back pain and ended up in hospital. I was pushing myself too hard and finally thought, what am I doing to myself? I can't go on like this."

Juggling competing demands is a classic trigger, but the energy of this one is slightly different. Stress gives off a higher frequency; we speed up, get more driven, try desperately to hold it all together, run from meeting to meeting, week to week. Work, children, families, partners, risk are all balls we have up in the air and almost always at some point or other these will get out of balance and drop.

The innocent questions posed by children can often be the wake-up calls that cut to the core of your own carelessness; sending your child to school in uniform when it was World Book Day as you were so busy you didn't read the slips from school. Taking the kids on holiday to Lapland on Xmas Eve and being so preoccupied with work that you forget to look at whether the passports are in date. Hands up - I have done both and I cannot tell you the guilt that caused me. Missed school plays, forgotten ingredients for the school cooking lesson, being routinely late for the school pick up are all common triggers.

Forgetting to drop the children off at nursery and leaving them in the back of the car is a little more extreme but there is not much I have not witnessed when working alongside stressed, juggling execs. As one client ruefully said in a session recently: "When my children were small they would rush in, full of energy, wanting to tell me all about their day.

I would tell them that daddy was busy, as I was always on my computer. What happens is they grow up and at some point they just don't come to tell you anything anymore". His share had quite an impact on the rest of the group and he made me think of a board director in his 50's who mentored me when I had just given birth to my second daughter Amy. He said "Nic, whatever you do don't get too driven at this point in your career. You can never get this time back. I hardly remember spending any time with my children when they were young as I was always at work, traveling abroad, working late and not present when I was home. I am making up for it now with my grandchildren, but it is something I deeply regret". In some ways if you get a wake-up call about your children when they are small then you are one of the lucky ones. The sadness is magnified when the realisation comes too late to do anything about it. In a stress state when we get driven something always has to give. It is our choice what that give is.

Whilst some of those I interviewed were still not making the money they might want, and they still had some practical challenges they wanted support with, they had no regrets. Other than that they didn't do it years before.

But it is not just our families that can provide the most powerful wake up calls; it can be the work itself. For most of us working to earn a living is a necessity, but if we are going to spend the inordinate amount of time we spend at work, we may as well do something we love; *with* and *for* those we love working alongside. Work that gives energy rather than takes it away: that rewards us with money for doing something that we excel at: that comes very naturally, effortlessly: that enables us to do something worthwhile for ourselves, for others or for the communities we live in. If we were to look at our work through this lens; then knowing ourselves, our strengths and what lights us up rather than what we have fallen into, or what other people have asked us to do, becomes an incredibly important exercise.

Knowing who we are is one of the most important foundations of change.

The Life changer

Sometime wake-up calls are the one offs that fall into the category of truly unpredictable events. The times when Life deals us a card that shocks us into looking at what really matters. A single event that no one would ever wish for or plan, that can turn out to be the point at which everything, and most importantly our perspective, changes; often forever, and for the better.

- "When my mum died I instantly lost the will to continue with my job. Everything was brought into perspective and I realised I didn't know what my values were anymore, but I knew I no longer held the same values and beliefs of the company I worked for, so could no longer continue living a lie."

- "I realised I was not immortal. In March 2014 I was diagnosed with Triple Negative Breast Cancer, this is not a hormonal cancer, there are fewer indicators for this type of cancer but one of the possible causes is stress. I needed six rounds of chemotherapy, 18 sessions of radiotherapy and a damn good wig"

Health and loss of it, is the one great leveller, the one thing we all have in common. As one inspiration of mine, Sophie Sabbage, says "we are all terminal, the difference between us is that people with a life limiting illness have been put on notice". Sophie was diagnosed with terminal lung cancer and multiple brain tumours back in Oct 2014 and given 6 months to live. She has busted all predictions and over the past 5 years has dedicated her life to living fully for herself, her young daughter and the husband she adores. She has also become the writer she always longed to become. Sophie has shared her terror with searing honesty in her bestselling book *The Cancer Whisper* (Coronet, 2016) which outlines the day-to-day practices and processes she herself taught others for years and that she practices herself so that it may inspire and help others who are living with cancer. She is the same person she always was, only brighter, bolder, and more fearless when it comes to sharing who she is. She is more connected to others perhaps, doing the same work she did, only now on a much bigger stage, a best-selling author with two books translated for audiences across the world who has made appearances on countless high profile TV, Radio shows and daily newspapers.

Her diagnosis was one you would not wish on anyone, her response to it has been nothing short of magnificent to watch.

I know from my work that Sophie is not alone. The thing about prospective or actual loss is that it can have the uncanny ability to change our relationship with time. It is the one thing that we cannot or should not take for granted, yet most of us do. But once the reality of our own mortality is brought into sharp focus, directly or indirectly through someone close to us, it often brings with it an unexpected gift: a desire to not mess about, to make the time count, to drop whatever excuses you made for not doing something and just go for it.

This type of wake-up call can go one of 2 ways. For Sophie it propelled her forward to achieve her life's work, on a far bigger stage. But for others it can do the exact opposite.

Sometimes doing and being more looks like booking that trip around the world you have always wanted to do, choosing to work less or indeed stopping work altogether.

I first met Sam Sedwill when we worked together at Bass Brewers. We stayed friends and kept in touch after she and her husband both left the organisation. We reconnected after I too left; by this time she was HR Director for a large med tech organisation and brought me in to support one of her senior execs when I started up my consulting business. It was after having worked together closely again for a couple of years that she told me that she had been diagnosed with breast cancer. I have never had anyone as close to me as Sam go through treatment for cancer. Her fragility and vulnerability were a shock at times to witness through those gruelling months of chemo.

Her attitude, beauty, determination, warmth and love that wrapped around her like a blanket were utterly inspiring. Sam recovered and returned to work within a year. She had previously only really had one setting when it came to work: full on. She is probably one of the most organised, efficient, competent and productive people I have ever worked alongside.

But she soon realised that running at the same pace was not going to work. After some time out, she joined another healthcare business as a consultant working 2 days a week. Changing the way she structured her work ensured she could give and share her talent in a way that also provided her with balance and quality time to live and stay well. Having come through this period of hardship Sam is happier, stronger, has such wisdom and somehow shines even brighter than ever before. As she said herself:

"The silver lining of being ill was that I changed the way I worked; I did the things that mattered, I said no to tasks that added no value, and I protected my time off. Although my confidence was knocked, I think I was actually more effective and definitely did not waste any of my work time.   However, I did feel different. In December 2016 I resigned and my husband and I took a four-month sabbatical in South America. It was a time to reflect, to celebrate and to get focused on the future. I now work for myself and have a different perspective on life: it's now about health and happiness, after all, what else is there?"

Would Sam have come to this without cancer?

Would I have set up a business on my own without an unplanned ending?

Who knows?

What is fact is that those things happened. Some things we don't choose - would not *want* to choose and yet they become catalysts for change. Providing an insight which strikes like a lightning bolt and transforms everything for the better.

But it does beg the question:

What if we could wake up without the mother of all wake-up calls?

What if all it took was to ask ourselves a series of questions?

I read recently a psychology paper on Trust written by Arthur Aron (and others), (Aron, 1997) where pairs of strangers were asked to explore 36 questions that require answers from the heart. The exercise tested how trust and connection can be built through disclosure. To quote the study's authors, "*One key pattern associated with the development of a close relationship among peers is sustained, escalating, reciprocal, personal self-disclosure.*"

Allowing ourselves to open up and be vulnerable with another person can be a challenge for most of us, so this exercise forces the issue and speeds it up. I use it in my coaching with pre-work that is designed to do exactly the same; start a process of enquiry, openness and trust. Asking the big questions, the deeper questions, which require a reveal of what usually gets hidden behind the veil of professionalism and guardedness also works in terms of bringing teams closer together. It works equally well for self-enquiry: if you let yourself answer in an unfiltered and honest way, it helps to bring what is already sitting underneath to the surface.

I have included a few of the questions by way of illustration from Arons' experiment in the action step below that you can try to answer for yourself. On their own these are powerful questions - the kind that we may rarely think to ask day-to-day or talk about with those closest to us at work or at home, let alone a complete stranger. They clarify who and what really matter, they require us to think more deeply; an essential pivot for change and from which focused, clear energy and direction can emerge.

If you are someone who likes to get ahead of the curve, and not afraid to ask the big questions, then some proactive, regular time for your own development outside of the day-to-day to think, reflect is likely to be something you have been or are drawn to. I have a great friend, Tamsin Chubb, who runs *Little French Retreat* deep in the wilds of the French countryside. I have been on retreat with Tamsin in India and stayed at her place many times. We also trained together in Denmark to master a coaching practice called Flow, which facilitates people to overcome a genuine challenge, by asking powerful questions from different perspectives. Both of us have since woven Flow into our coaching and team work, to powerful effect. But what really makes Tamsin special is her ability to create a peaceful space that others can step into in order to relax, open up and rest. Most people that go on retreat with Tamsin end up saying they had no idea how tired they are until they went to see her and took the time to actually stop. It is amazing what we can see when we rest our minds and come home.

It is not unlike why many come for Exec Coaching: sometimes because there has been some feedback or an issue that the individual has been asked to do something about in order to get to the next promotional level. But often because work has sped up to such a frequency that they can no longer see the wood for the trees.

It doesn't have to be that way.

We don't have to wait until the wheels come off to make changes.

Courage, dear heart

Change starts with noticing. It starts with a commitment to personal enquiry; to asking the big questions to see what is changing within and around us. We have a choice to do this proactively but of course if we don't, the beauty is we can always rely on a wake-up call.

So, my learnings on the power of the wake-up call:

1) The catalyst for change can come in 2 ways: from a place of vision; something more you want to go for or achieve that pulls you forward. Or it can come through purposefulness from pain - an ending or challenge so fundamental that it forces you to re-evaluate what really matters - and, what, as a result, this means you want to do and how you respond.

   Allowing yourself to stop, to tune in to the whispers and the disquiet is the first step. This may come from one or more events, or simply from the curiosity to go deeper and see what is there.

2) Take the time to regularly stop and listen to this will move you forward quicker in the long run. From a place of honesty good things have a chance to come, so we will look at how to review the events that have brought you to this point - how to notice

the signs, take the learning and most importantly decide what, if anything you actually want to *do* about it.

3) Taking action and making it happen is where the hard work starts: where focus and discipline is required. This is where the story really begins to take shape and a whole new set of challenges, fears and blocks can emerge. For the action oriented like me, this can be the part of the process you feel most comfortable in. But rush into solutions too quickly and patterns can have a habit of repeating themselves. So you may have a plan but not one that really solves the issues you face.

So before we get stuck in to *the how* it pays to press pause, reflect and look inward.

Action Step 1

If you want to start the enquiry about what you really want, first take time to answer the following questions:

- What would constitute a perfect day for you?

- What is the greatest accomplishment of your life?

- For what in your life do you feel most grateful?

- If a crystal ball could tell you the truth about yourself, your life, the future or anything else, what would you want to know?

- If you knew that in one year you would die suddenly, would you change anything about the way you are now living? Why?

Chapter 2: Looking back

"When it's all finished you will discover it was never random"

- **Unknown**

I am a great believer in the importance of looking back in order to move forward. In my work with organisations and teams who run fast to achieve a lot, it is the one thing they often neglect to do as much as they know they should. As a result, they often suffer from a collective blind spot that requires some intention and regular time specifically organised to slow down, regroup, reflect and re-align.

There is power and purpose in regularly running a Review: to see what can be learned so that the cycles of doing the same thing over and over and getting the same result are curtailed. So that wasted effort, time, money is minimised. So that we do better.

What can get in the way of this is our relationship to failure and blame. In his book Black Box Thinking (Syed, 2016); Matthew Syed illustrates powerfully through many direct examples, and, in, particular, by contrasting two of the most safety critical industries in the world today: healthcare and aviation – two businesses who operate at extremes of a continuum. The core of his argument is simple: The airline industry place two virtually indestructible black boxes in every aircraft; one which records the instructions sent to the on-board computer systems, and one which records the conversations and sounds in the cockpit. He argues the success of this industry is driven by the ruthless focus they place on examining failure in order to prevent future risk and serious incident. In his book he shares the practices and structures created to ensure full disclosure and sharing of information in a simple form across the industry. At the other end of the scale, he studies the Healthcare industry where it is estimated that preventable harm (misdiagnosis, dispensing the wrong drugs, operating on the wrong part of the body etc.) is estimated to be the 3rd biggest killer in the USA behind heart disease and cancer. He argues that many errors have predictable patterns, and that with open reporting and honest evaluation these errors could be spotted and prevented from happening again as in aviation, but that all too often this does not happen.

At heart he argues that this is a cultural issue, led by technical experts who, whilst human, are not permitted to fail because of the demands of the ego and/or the culture of fear that exists in these institutions about speaking up and owning mistakes. An example of what he calls 'closed loop learning'. What is clear to him, and without doubt something I have experience of personally is that many of our public services are led by smart, motivated and caring people; as are the institutions and people who audit them, but according to a recent House of Commons select committee when things go wrong and investigations do happen, these people seem mostly preoccupied with blame and avoiding financial liability.

The difference comes down to purpose of the enquiry: How did events play out so that we do better vs. who is to blame so that heads roll. Reviewing at its best is an honest enquiry into what happened so that the 'what' and the 'how' can be improved. It requires a rational, objective approach and an openness to what part we played. This requires us to take individual accountability and look for what can be learned and shared so that collectively we do better.

There is no difference at a personal level. Something illustrated beautifully in a quote that M Sayed shares by Heather Hanbury, a former head teacher of a High School in London. She asked parents, tutors and other role models to talk about how they had failed and what they had learned, so that her students could get a realistic feel for how success happens. She said:

"You are not born with fear of failure. It's not an instinct. It's something that grows and develops in you as you get older. Very young children have no fear of failure at all. They have great fun trying new things and learning very fast. Our focus here is on failing well, on being good at failure. What I mean by this is taking a risk and then learning from it if it doesn't work.

There is no point in failing then dealing with it by pretending it didn't happen or blaming someone else. That would be a wasted opportunity to learn more about yourself and perhaps to identify gaps in your skills, experiences or qualifications. Once you have identified the learning you can then take the action to make a difference."

If only we could retain this love of learning. If only we could change our relationship with failure and see it as an opportunity rather than something to be dreaded and avoided at all costs.

What if we could look back with a sense of openness rather than criticism and judgement?

The latter really does go to the heart of learning. To be able to step back and look at what 'is' and what happened to reach that state objectively. To see the ups and downs without the hook of blame. To retain the same spirit of openness that can transcend age, if we let it.

Write down your own story and you are likely to see patterns that repeat. I use my own reflections as an illustration and after you have read it, if you want, give it a go for yourself.

So what happened?

Courage, dear heart

My first taste of failure came with my A levels. Looking back, boys, going out, having fun, working weekends to earn money to fund my social life and wardrobe temporarily took over and when it came to exam time the lack of attention to detail I had placed in my preparation came home to roost. I thought I could sail through as I had done before, and I found I could not. I had, as my teacher had repeatedly warned me, been burning the candle at both ends. The grades were nowhere near those I had been predicted and I didn't get into the university I wanted to attend. I remember that feeling of sinking dread when I looked at that slip of paper, and what I imagined my dad would have to say about it.

Whilst I feared the worst, he was remarkably supportive and matter of fact. So were my teachers, and with a little help from my tutor at 6th form college I got a deferral to Leeds to read Business Studies, Marketing and French. I decided to make good use of the unexpected year off working a ski season in a hotel in Gstaad Switzerland. I was 18 with a big adventure in front of me; the chance to live away from home, learn a new language and work alongside a bunch of amazing people from around the world I had never met. Youthful exuberance and an ability to make the most of just about anything, my attitude and sense of adventure got me through. It was an awesome year that I had not planned for and I never looked back. But I had learnt my first lesson the hard way: that if there is something you want within a specific time period, then preparation really does help. And if you want that result to be one that you repeat to a high quality then there is no other way around it, you need to do the work.

Fast forward 10 years. I was 28 and working in the Marketing department of Bass Brewers in the Midlands. I had been promoted to my very first senior manager position and a month later unexpectedly found out I was pregnant with my eldest daughter Ella. I have to say that making the decision with James to go for it and bring Ella into the world was the single best decision we have ever made. She changed everything. She certainly changed me – and for the better. It was whilst on maternity leave that I first remember thinking that I wanted to be a teacher. My heart had opened. I wanted to be around Ella more, I wanted to do meaningful work, for others, and quite simply I love to learn so it made sense to do what I love. I looked into what it would take to retrain but concerns about money took precedence. I put the whispers back in a box and went back to work part time.

Fast forward another 10 years and the whispers were back. By now I had 2 children, James and I had separated, amicably, and we were co-parenting together - as we still do. After my second maternity leave, I had decided to throw myself back into work fully. The focus, hard work, a side step out of marketing and some additional strategy projects, mergers and acquisitions work had paid off: I was promoted quickly into my first Senior Exec role as Sales MD. It was a turnaround role where I had little technical experience that was to be both the most pivotal of my career and cement my learning and practice of how to lead. I absolutely loved it and the people I worked alongside and for. My only wish is that I had stayed in it for longer. As it was, within 2 years I was asked by the CEO to come back as Director of Marketing and take the role I had longed for when my career began. I had a new team to shape and develop, a new set of challenges to get under the skin of, a new set of people to work alongside and external relationships to build, a substantial engagement challenge to work through, a new vision and strategy to create and a massive opportunity to make a difference quickly with the insights and practices I now brought with me from Sales. In some ways it ticked all the boxes (all these things still do actually) but I knew that my heart was no longer in advertising or drinks. 15 years in one company had provided me with some amazing opportunities to lead, train, facilitate, create and innovate for which I am still hugely grateful.

I also worked with very warm, interesting, funny, engaged and engaging teams who kept me emotionally locked in.

At the time, stepping outside of the organisation and away from these people seemed like a big deal: walking into another job that was exactly the same to lead a team selling something else did not appeal. Doing what I really wanted to do seemed an impossible dream that I had no clue how to make real. For the first time in my career I had everything on paper that I had always wanted but my heart was no longer in it and I felt utterly stuck.

The first opportunity to leave came within a year, when the organisation needed to cut costs: an exercise that I had significant input on. I can remember sitting at my desk with one of my colleagues the morning of the consultation meeting. We were required to submit which role or roles we were interested in. He asked me which I was going for and I remember looking at him completely blank. The truth was I didn't want any of them. An hour later I was sat with my boss and the HR Lead, both of whom I adored. They looked at me expectantly and smiled, "So, what role would you like to apply for, Nic?" I knew exactly what they both wanted me to do and I found myself ticking the box for the VP of Innovation role.

I walked out of the meeting slightly dazed and burst into tears in the car park.

That moment is as vivid now as it was then, and it taught me what fear could make me do.

Or **not** do.

It would keep me safe in a job that others wanted me to do but that I didn't want. I had made a mistake in not taking a risk and I knew it. It took me 6 months to have that conversation with my boss and, for the second time, contrary to the way my mind had it pictured, when I did, he was amazingly supportive, and I felt the burden of pretence lift from my shoulders.

What did I learn?

My Mindset could both enable me to recover quite brilliantly while at others times hold me back from acting on and telling the truth. My own experience and the personal development I pursued to try to understand fear more taught me 3 things:

1) Fear loves to catastrophize. It predicts and it exaggerates. It will paint a very vivid picture of what is going to happen, placing great emphasis on the worst-case scenario. It also judges. Judges, everyone, all of the time, with the most severe criticism saved for ourselves, and what others will think of us.

2) When fear is in the driving seat it severely limits our capacity to think clearly, to see possibilities and to open up to others. Fear narrows, limits, drives short term and reactive responses. In it we play small and

show up as the version of ourselves we (and others) least like.

3) Sadly, we can be the last one to know we are in its grip when we stop listening and stop noticing the warning signs. But if there is one thing you can be sure of, it is that the warning signs will just keep coming: louder and louder until they finally stop us in our tracks.

At which point it is a good time to press pause and start getting real.

Action Step:

Draw your timeline. Think about the significant events and how they unfolded. You can do this as you look back over your life or if you prefer, the last year.

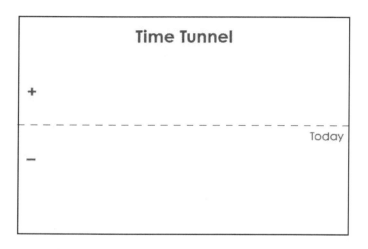

This step is about honesty and marking the chronological order of events in your life as they unfolded.

Take your time.

Concentrate on the flow: what were the highs, what were the lows, the wins and successes and the times that felt anything but and where were the pivot points as you look back where everything changed?

At this point just draw the flow as you remember.

Chapter 3: Telling the Truth

"The truth will set you free, but first it will piss you off"

- **Gloria Steinem**

I have read a lot of books on innovation over the years, most of which aligned in the school of thought that making mistakes is not just a good thing but absolutely essential. When we look with the benefit of hindsight through the vast number of case studies on the subject, whether in fields of science or consumer brands, breakthroughs rarely happen without a succession of failures.

Meaning that the key to successful innovation is much more likely to be born from a deeply practical process of trial and error, combined with a spirit of playfulness, curiosity and commitment to learn and continually do better, than it is sitting on coloured bean bags blue sky thinking. As Sir James Dyson says, "failures feed the imagination; you can't have one without the other". For me there is a fundamental truth that getting to the heart of the issue and the willingness to make mistakes in the pursuit of solving it builds corporate insight and wisdom which, if captured and shared with others, drives transformation.

This of course makes sense but is, in reality, easier to say than do – particularly when our ego either individually or corporately is tied up with 'looking good'. Getting to the heart of the issue means admitting you have an issue in the first place, whether this be as a team, organisation or industry. And in my experience, it can be surprisingly hard for some at the very top (or those aspiring to be promoted by them) to admit. I was contacted by an HR Director who had been referred to me, and her opening line was "I saw your website and what you do, the thing is we don't have an issue..." and then went on to share very honestly about the insights and feedback she was picking up. The company was hitting plan, so she did not have an issue with the numbers, which is great and of course a very tangible marker of success. However, under the surface, she could see there were people issues bubbling up, signs of disengagement and several Board members who were technically very proficient but who lacked basic skills in listening, communication and feedback. If not addressed, she feared all three would impact future success should some of their top talent decide to leave as some had indicated they were about to do.

She could see something that some of the Board could not.

The challenge for her was how to land the feedback with those more senior than her; how to support the Board to become more attuned to their people, and communicate more openly as a group, in terms of both what was going well and what was not. What was clear immediately to me is that she did have at least two issues. Firstly, the Board was in denial about a capability gap and secondly, she as HR Director was fearful about telling them.

Transformation of any kind, whether it be corporate innovation or personal, I think is inextricably linked to truth telling: the openness to proactively seek out what is not working alongside what is clearly brilliant, combined with the willingness to share honestly and freely so that we and others might learn and collectively do better.

Truth telling is pragmatic, gritty and real. It drives innovation and is a foundation for success.

Courage, dear heart

Embrace it and you will do better and so will others around you.

Truth telling is also hard. And often uncomfortable. Especially when it involves taking a look in the mirror; to face into what is going on within us rather than burying it or pointing the finger elsewhere.

I had the most beautiful example of this shared by a colleague, someone who is absolutely brilliant at what she does. A shining star who didn't feel it underneath:

"Life was good. Then our company got bought out and there followed a messy 9 months really of taking a bit of an ego battering. All of the people around me slowly left and my inputs were not really valued as the new company was in a very different place. Much longer story, but I think now I can see it wasn't personal – just one company taking over another and doing things their way. But at the time, I felt battered by them. I always struggle to get my point of view across, but I was fighting to do this, then getting knocked back with meetings carrying on without me there.

So I eventually left, but I don't think I realised quite the impact it had on my confidence. I needed to be at my prime confidence to make a difference in the new organisation I moved to. I wasn't and over time there it got worse with a very domineering line manager who only really knew how to do things her own way and wasn't open to any other. I had numerous failed attempts at trying to influence but eventually I gave up. The weird thing is I didn't do any of that consciously. I just fell into doing the easiest thing. It was an "easy job", it didn't challenge me, and my home life therefore was great as I could always be around for my family. So whilst I wasn't fulfilled, I would say that on the surface I felt content. I think there were other clues there that I wasn't confident at all, but I chose to ignore it and see them as not connected or relevant. The biggest example I can give you there is that I started having weird panic attacks when I was driving. Not major ones, but enough to make me pull off/pull over and have to calm myself down. Just seemed to come from nowhere and I would say probably got worse. I felt quite ashamed of it, like a weakness, so I just didn't talk to anyone about it."

It is hard to admit to ourselves a truth, let alone anyone else when we judge ourselves so harshly.

I have been guilty of this one myself. I run review processes all the time with Exec teams in order to embed learning and reassure them honestly that their mistakes will be the making of them. I believe that to be true and my experience of facilitating these sessions over and over shows they always are.

But when it comes to my personal life and I have made a mistake; particularly when it comes to not seeing the downside of someone's character, then I give myself a really hard time:

"You should know better", "your intuition (that I am so often told is a strength) has failed", "you have failed", "you got it wrong and trusted someone you should not have".

This is how judgments generally play out in the mind, harsh accusations accompanied by a list of how things, others and you should have been different. Now the truth is, being open, trusting and being someone who sees the good in people is a trait I would rather have. It enables me to connect easily with people and help them see the amazing things that often they cannot. On balance it serves me well. And yes, sometimes I have trusted people who have hurt me.

It happens.

Taking the learning (and there always was one!) without the judgment, blame and finger pointing is what this process is about. Doesn't matter whether the finger pointing is at other people or you. Either way it is never helpful.

So truth telling is about 2 things:

Exposing the repeat patterns and trigger events, being honest about the wins and the challenges.

Being clear about what part you played in creating those highs and lows. The things we did or did not do in the run up to a pivot point of change. If in doubt, ask for some help from someone you trust; it can help to have the eyes of another to keep you really honest.

Here are my own reflections:

Truth telling: The mistake and the learning

The truth is I had stopped listening to myself. I was driving myself harder and harder. I am very results driven, I am wired to do the very best I can for others, to be, and be known as, good at what I do.

But I was taking it to extremes which was coming at significant cost. I was suffering from severe backache at this time which those around me at work and at home knew well. I had cortisone injections in my spine and was warned by the consultant that if they failed to work, the next step would be surgery. The conflict I was feeling inside was showing up in my body. I was in pain and frequently tearful. There wasn't anything physically wrong with me, it was stress and the truth is the moment I closed this chapter of my life, the pain stopped, and I have not needed to see a doctor or osteopath since.

I was not taking responsibility for making a plan or asking for help to create one. I didn't let anyone in to what was really going on other than my partner. I closed in trying to figure it all out myself which limited my options and meant that when the offer came from him, I took it as it was the only one I had or could see as possible. In this respect I was the architect of one aspect of the predicament I found myself in: I had not done any preparation on the 'How' and for the second time in my life after a fall, after I had dusted off the damage to my ego, my attitude would be the thing that saw me through.

But great results generally require a positive Mindset, talent and preparation. Two out of three isn't enough.

Truth Telling: What I wanted

I wanted to be around more for my girls. The balance of my time was with the girls whilst they were in pre-school when I worked part time, but work had absolutely taken a priority during their primary years. Ella was at this point 11 and Amy 10. Time was slipping by all too quickly and I knew that as they hit their teenage years they would in some ways need me even more. I felt guilty and the girls were starting to voice that they wanted me working and living in one place. Success in one domain was coming at a huge price in another and it was one I could no longer bear.

I needed and wanted to change. But I was scared, and whilst driven by fear I was not taking responsibility for what it would take to create that change. What you can be sure of eventually is that if you don't take responsibility, someone else might. The relationship ending when it came hurt. It hurt because I wasn't in control of it, because it left me exposed in a tough situation that I had not planned for.

However, as I quickly found out, this pivot point in my life was to be the making of me. This was not lost on my ex-partner. "You have grown more in the past few months than you did in years with me" he remarked ruefully a couple of months down the line. He always was, and I'm sure is, very insightful and it was absolutely true. I had grown - which was down to me, and my response to this challenge. Realising that actually made moving forward much easier.

We will look more at what to do with this insight in the chapters that follow but for now:

1) Writing down how events played out, the chronology of how events happened is a hugely important process. It helps us to see the patterns of behaviour, the sequence, how one action or decision led to another and what, with hindsight, was missed. It is fact based; "what is so", with no judgement about who or what was right or wrong. What it showed me was that, as is often the way, history had repeated itself, the calling had been with me for a long time and the significant men in

my life like my father, my girls' father James, the bosses who I respect, admire and trust all share a level headedness, pragmatism and very thoughtful approach. Contrary to my fear, they were also my biggest supporters when I needed it for which I am very grateful.

2) Telling the truth about what you had to do with what played out is essential if you don't want to play victim and waste time and energy blaming anyone and everyone else for how you feel. This was not one of those events that I could not have predicted. It didn't come from nowhere. The signs were there, the triggers were building one by one. I was disconnected from my heart, my body and what was realistically going to work for my girls. To tell the truth, you have to put the ego aside and get real; preferably to others but most importantly to yourself.

3) Who and what really matters. This is generally a truth that comes from the heart. Everyone is different. We all have our own stories, experiences, values that run deep, people in our lives who ground us and make us realise what it's all for when

we forget. Purpose is just remembering who and what they are.

Once you have it, you stand a much greater chance in taking your next step towards you at your best, rather than your worst.

Action Step

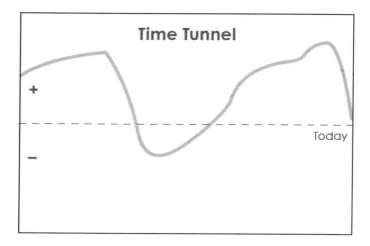

Look back at the story of how events unfolded. You can do this exercise on your own or with someone else.

If you pick one of the pivotal moments from your past where the time line changes.

As you look back with hindsight, what were the significant events and wake up calls you remember experiencing in the run up to the pivotal change?

What was the truth about when the wake-up calls started?

What was the part you were playing in it all?

Chapter 4: Tricks the Mind can play

"What if I fall, but my darling what if you fly"

- **Erin Hanson**

There are some great books out there which centre of self-awareness and consciousness. Books which examine the voice inside our head, the endless chatter that goes on between our ears; commenting, analysing, imagining, worrying about what has happened, what could happen, what should happen, what we did or didn't do, should have done or said, what others should have done or said, what we have got to do, what might happen if we do it, what we think of others and what they do or will think of us…..

The Untethered Soul (Singer, 2009) is a beautiful book I read last year on retreat in India and absolutely loved. The first chapter talks about the voice inside your head, and the importance of knowing that you are not the voice. You are the viewer who sits in the armchair of your mind listening to it comment on everything, all the time. It helps to get to know the voice but also to know that there is not much to be gained from taking much notice of it or trying to figure everything out.

Why does it exist? To keep us safe. The human brain contains a very small centre called the amygdala. This is the source of our fight, flight and freeze responses. Its purpose is to analyse events in milliseconds and tell us what to do in response. It remembers danger and predicts what will happen so that we can avoid death or injury. So from an evolutionary point of view, it is a part of our brain that has been essential to our survival as a species. But as with most brilliant things, it also has its downsides.

You will notice if you choose to tune into that voice in your head, that it is constant.

You will notice it will dial up a notch in certain situations, with certain people or times of the day, but it is always present whether you notice it or not. It creates an exhausting commentary that has tremendous power which if left unchallenged and, unchecked, drives us to spend time in one of two camps: the past which we can no longer do anything about or the future; painting scenarios that may or may not come to fruition. Which, of course, robs us of our focus, our peace of mind, our attention to what is right in front of us and the quality of connection we have with the people we most care about. The mind talk equivalent of watching two people sat opposite each other in a restaurant where both are engrossed in their phones, distracted in their own virtual worlds. The joy and connection of talking, laughing, sharing, enjoying the moment, seeing and being seen by another human in real life being parked in favour of a solitary relationship with superficial and instantly forgettable wittering's on line. A state that is slightly sad to witness, not to mention a monumentally pointless waste of time.

I first became aware of this voice in my head in my early 30's via a Leadership Mindsets training at work. As a trainer and coach, it is without doubt one of the most beautiful moments imaginable when, like the flick of a switch, you see the light go on behind the eyes of another. When they see something about themselves they had not seen before. When suddenly events make sense in a new light. When an insight lands and transforms both what they do and how. It never fails to send chills through me when I see it. Which is exactly how I felt and must have looked when I went through that training.

What it sparked was a passion to learn more, to experience more, and to go deeper. For many years I trained for my own personal development with *More to Life* and then for a while as a coach, trainer of self- esteem to support people to unlock the unconscious drivers of the mind, let go of self-judgment and build greater self-confidence. Something I did until I had it.

The first lesson I learnt from the teaching was related to the events and people that can influence us as children that have the power to shape our beliefs and behaviour as adults. Now this aspect of self-development and analysis is not for everyone, but as someone who has been drawn to understand psychology I personally found it fascinating. I do believe I gained a greater understanding of the patterns playing out in my relationships that went back a very long way; to the dynamics I observed and experienced at home. It was, in some ways, from a very rational standpoint helpful to step back and see the patterns in a new light.

But it does not change anything given that we can never go back. There is very little to be gained from blaming anyone or pinning everything that has not happened as we might have wished on someone or something from our past. All we can do is make peace with it and ensure that in the future the choices we make are from a clearer, more informed space. This is the same principle we looked at in Chapter 2: when the energy is focused on doing better, we do better. When the energy is focused on interrogating why things are as they are, of uncovering fault or blame, there is perhaps a short-term pay off of knowing who or what started it but much good rarely comes. If anything, it just leads to more disconnect from those seen as 'at fault'.

The second thing I learnt was making the invisible visible has power. Speaking up and giving a voice to issues not discussed is the only way to work through them. Bringing fears out into the light, through the act of saying them out loud to another, often has the funny effect of cutting them off at the knees; of making you realise that what you have carried as a truth in your head may in fact be false in reality or at best a projection that, with objectivity, cannot be verified or predicted as a certainty. I have had countless clients say to me that they have revealed issues, concerns or events to me in our sessions that they have never spoken about to others, not even those closest to them. Often because they have simply been too ashamed to. But the act of saying something out loud that has long been buried in the recesses of our minds has a strange way of freeing us up. All that is required is trust: that we are in a safe space to be vulnerable, and that whatever we say, we will not to be judged.

There is however, one point of caution for me: going over and over the past, analysing and spending too much time on the false beliefs and drivers of the mind can merely serve to reinforce them. As one hugely experienced trainer who I did have the privilege of working alongside and learning from said to me one day: "Nic, you know I have come to realise our minds are a bit of a mess: trying to unravel and analyse *too* much is pointless.

Ultimately what matters is that we know we can choose how we want to be".

I agree with him and that choice can start at any time.

About a month ago I attended a public lecture organised by PIER on safeguarding the role emergency services play in collaborating to keep our communities, vulnerable people and children safe. I was there with a client because I work across Police, Fire and NHS and collaboration between these services is a key theme. The speaker was Nazir Afzal, OBE, lawyer, former Chief Prosecutor who led the successful prosecution of the perpetrators of the child sex abuse scandal in Rotherham and several high-profile celebrity sexual predators. He shared a number of personal learnings and insights from his own experience which I headline below:

1) **Leadership beliefs:** What do you care about? What are you going to champion? Will you stand up and support people? Will you tackle the stuff in the too difficult pile? Will you do what is right?

Nazir talked about the need to challenge for what is right: how we need to speak up more for others who cannot. This means putting yourself on the line.

He was sacked for speaking up on *Question Time* about some of the underlying issues and drivers behind the Manchester Arianne Grande concert bombing. At the time he was working as Chief Exec for the Police and Crime Commissioners. Now this is my view only, but it shows what can happen when politics gets in the way of saying what needs to be said; of standing up for truth not a party line. But every ending always has a start, and he is now free to stand up and say exactly what he feels needs to be said and does so to powerful effect.

2) **Response to issues: How do you react in a moment of crisis or conflict?** In his experience of public life, echoed by the work of Mathew Sayed, Nazir felt that the initial reaction is usually "heads must roll". What generally then happens is that our Public institutions put in new and more process only to find that the new process doesn't actually work. By which time the attention has usually shifted onto something or someone else. What we need to do is to shine a light on the behaviours. Be transparent. Focusing on continuous improvement and prevention require us to be open and talk about what the problematic issues are and our

experiences of what *is* working so that we drive change.

3) **Listening:** How do you know what is really going on? Listen. Listen to what went wrong. Nazir talked about how he used to start his meetings with his team not with the minutes but by what went wrong last week. He also talked about the importance of listening to the individual. Giving them the respect and care to listen to their story. Sometimes this is all the closure they need.

4) **Engaging with others: How do you inspire confidence?** Confidence comes from being highly competent. This is how you build confidence with others as well as getting out there and talking to people. Ask for their ideas, their help and make it easy for people to come forward and express themselves.

5) **Resilience: How do you take care of yourself?** With any position of influence or responsibility, or any time you put yourself out there, you need to be prepared to open yourself up to critics, hate mail, and abuse. He referenced that whilst leading the prosecution against the mainly British Asian gang in Rotherham, he received 17k email hate letters, was

the target for English Defence League (EDL) demonstrations outside his home and the subject of on-line fake news. If you are going to cope under such pressure then support is key: you need to surround yourself with a great team who will protect you, handle the emails you don't need to see, take care of communications when you need it and make sure you have someone to share with (peers, emotional support). Wrap around support is as important for any leader in positions of responsibility as it is for victims.

As a consultant I listened to the talk he gave, and the leadership principles he set out with clarity, and agree wholeheartedly: both the importance of being clear about who you are and what you stand for, speaking up about issues with honesty, of listening to build trusting relationships, of behaviours over process every time, and of the importance of surrounding yourself with the very best people and the humility to know when you need support. It is 100% aligned to the principles and practices I teach.

Inside of me it also woke up the 12-year-old girl who had been a victim of sexual assault. I dropped Nazir a note after his speech on Twitter and thanked him. I had now quite literally put my experience out there publicly to a load of people I didn't know.

As I listened to him that night that is what I wanted to do. That the only power it had over me was that it was and had been for decades a secret, never discussed by me or those closest to me who thought it best to move on and leave it in the past. It got tucked away, a fair bit of the detail wiped from my memory and yet I have always known full well that the trial, perhaps surprisingly as much as the event, had a profound impact which echoed through the years. One of the reasons that I used to feel heavy sickness of dread before going on stage before a big presentation, particularly one where I was there to talk about myself, had its roots right here. When stood in front of a sea of eyes staring at me, a memory would be unlocked: I am transported back to the courtroom, I can see the judge, the barristers, I can feel a sea of eyes on me, I am being asked questions, I am small, I can feel the fear of not knowing what to say, of freezing up, closing down, of feeling unable to say or do anything but cry.

For years I would work hard to find props and rituals to make me look more confident when it was the last thing I felt. I would prepare endlessly what I was going to say, repeating it over and over again the night before, memorising my words right up to going on stage. My team would laugh at me, but I always had a new dress, heels, the obligatory conference spray tan and red lipstick. If I felt nervous and small inside, I was determined not to look it. It got me through but involved a fair bit of effort, and inside I wasn't at peace.

One pivot point for change was a presentation skills course. I was asked to prepare a 10-minute presentation about something personal to share with the group during the course. I decided to face into it and present on my fear of presenting. Not why, but simply that I carried a very heavy burden of fear.

So that is what I shared, my worst fear was confirmed and I burst into tears.

Embarrassment was short lived and was traded for a weight lifted and surprising feeling of freedom. I can still see their faces now as I write this. Bless them. They really didn't see it coming at all and had no idea what so ever that this is how I had always felt. Because I never talked about it; I hid it, tried to work around it. Which is the thing about fear - when held in tightly, it simply eats on the host and slowly but surely disconnects us from those around us at work and at home.

Supporting others has taught me many things, the most important perhaps being our shared humanity. What I have come to realise is we have all got something: memories, events often from that important time between childhood and adolescence, some seemingly insignificant, that have surprising echoes decades later. I have coached MDs who still hate reading off auto cue as it reminds them of being a child reading and stumbling over words at the front of the class. Or senior execs who still hate presenting to groups of people as it reminds them of speaking in the class with a foreign accent that the other kids used to take the mickey out of, or another who was having difficulty overcoming the challenging behaviour of one individual until the moment he realised that his reaction was actually being triggered by a memory of being bullied: something that had nothing to do with the individual at all.

Whilst on the outside we might look like we have it all sussed because we may have been elevated to a position of responsibility or because we may well possess qualities that others admire. But events, conversations, interactions large and small can stick with us and drive a prediction in the mind that whatever happened then will surely happen again and make us feel as stupid, powerless and ashamed in the moment as we did when a child. What others see on the outside is rarely what it feels like on the inside.

Understanding that helps to not put anyone else on a pedestal or put ourselves down.

We've all got something.

With the big, significant events that may have driven a belief or a fear for a very long time, I think talking it through and saying it out loud does help. There are many professionals out there who work with specific traumas. It took me until I was 40 to properly unpack what I had locked inside. I did it with a couple of people close to me, but it took another six years to open up and really deal with it once and for all, but better late than never. Often fears just get trapped inside us as children in what we are told and the behaviours we witness around us: little things that were said or done in a moment of carelessness can stick with us for decades, subconsciously shaping the adults we become. Being conscious of these events and being able to cut the invisible threads that bind us to them is a huge relief.

Sometimes though, admitting to fear can itself be the issue we grapple with most.

I get to see this play out in every Exec Coaching engagement. Each and every one marks the beginning of a new relationship; of openness and honesty, of unfolding, of unravelling past patterns, challenges and wants often spoken out loud to another for the first time. Each one creates a space of stillness and reflection; of safety to drop all masks and pretence, where anything that needs to be said can be, of unwavering encouragement, positivity and support alongside challenge that keeps us honest, accountable and moving forward. And of course, a fair bit of laughter. Learning, like so many other things in life and work, is so much more powerful when there is space for playfulness and fun. I received this testimonial from one client at the end of the coaching engagement:

"When we started, I was in a pretty dark place, lots of physical and emotional pain - even if I wasn't ready to admit it. The easy option would have been to walk away. With your coaching and support I truly believe the rainbows have returned. Some days are sunshine, some are rain but the clouds always clear away.....I have regained my confidence, stepped back into a strong leadership role, and am once again driving through transformational change."

My client might have contemplated walking away but she didn't, highlighting the most important aspects of all, which are two sides of the same coin: vulnerability and bravery. The willingness to go look in the dark places, to open up, to risk people seeing who you are, to share what you feel, what you really think. Vulnerability takes bravery, and both are the best ingredients for transformation and growth I know.

But let's be real: vulnerability, opening ourselves up is scary and fear sits at the heart of what stops us from doing the very things we most want and are capable of.

Which brings me to the purpose of looking at Mindset: which for me is so that we do better. That with greater awareness and determination, we can help ensure that the predictions and judgements of the mind can be understood, overcome, and an entirely new set of outcomes created. And in doing so be more of who we really are, at heart.

The purpose of examining our Mindset is not to master a process. It is not to go around in circles, analysing it to death and reinforcing our fears and the pathways in our brain that harden and narrow our responses.

This requires a commitment to moving forward.

I have met and worked alongside leaders - many talented good, caring and self-aware people. People whose work is dedicated to clarity, connection and service to the community, but who in spite of outward appearances simply don't get on. Power is always the most interesting of dynamics that is most often left unspoken, and one that will render a team paralysed when it is unclear, or where power sits where others in the team resent it being held. This is the domain of politics and where it exists, and agendas are unspoken or hidden: a team will always struggle to get clear on how best to move their organisation forward.

They will also struggle where process has become more important than being sharp on behaviours and results. When looking inward takes over from keeping one's eye firmly fixed on moving forward for the people who actually matter on the outside of the organization. Whenever there is a lack of alignment in purpose or power, dysfunction will perpetuate.

There is nothing wrong with a good process; one that is clear, simple and supports the result, goal or vision but not process that is an end or an industry in itself. My experience of working with over processed organisations is that it drives people to just go through the motions. They will do what they are told, filling out forms, regurgitating a script, mechanically repeating a practice because that is just what we do around here, or it was designed by someone of such perceived importance that it can never be challenged. Over time this sucks out energy, engagement and accountability. And the moment you drain the ingredients that drive pace, innovation and ideas you stifle progress. People will continue to do what they have always done and waste an inordinate amount of energy justifying policies and procedures that are often disconnected from the people and service delivery that actually matters.

So that is a long way to say, when it comes to Mindset, go into it with a purpose to move forward. If you go into it to master a process, to analyse and keep analyzing, you may find yourself very aware of the theory but still going round in circles.

And as a great teacher of mine, Atarangi Muru says, "Done correctly, once is enough". For any kind of deep work that is designed to get to the heart of the matter and shift energy, I would 100% agree with her.

Action Step

You can do this exercise on your own or with someone else if it will help to keep you objective and honest.

Think about a time when you experienced a real challenge. Taking one from your timeline or perhaps one you would like to work on now:

What fears do you/have you had?

What have you done to avoid feeling them?

What do you want to be different now?

Chapter 5: Mastering Mindset

"Everything can be taken from a man but one thing: the last of the human freedoms - to choose one's attitude in any given set of circumstances, to choose one's way."

- **Viktor Frankl, *Man's Search for Meaning***

I honestly think understanding the role that Mindset plays in determining our own happiness, connection to others and the results we create has been the most fundamental and transformative learning of my career. Understanding its existence, as we saw in the previous chapter, is key. But once you know you what it is, what do you do with it? How can you shift it?

This awareness, in addition to a framework and a language to help me understand and articulate my Mindset, was life changing at home and at work. As is the way of things, the more aware I became of the link between my own Mindset, behaviour and outcomes, the more adept I became in noticing and calling out the behaviours and language in others. Noticing and shifting mindset and engagement in teams unlocks energy, pace, momentum and results. You know the difference between someone who wants to learn; to give all they can, who wants to be there and someone who doesn't; whose heart is no longer in it.

You know the difference between really *wanting* to do something and, at the other extreme, feeling that you *have* to do something: going through the motions in body but not in spirit.

You know the difference between feelings of clarity and confidence and feelings of stress which you can feel irrespective of the gravity of the situation you find yourself in.

Managing Mindset is about two things: noticing and alignment. Being conscious of who you are, what you want, why and acting in alignment with that. Even in the times when faced with difficulty, in a set of circumstances we did not want and that we may not be in control of or have influence over. We own the choice as to how we respond, how we act, how we want to be. We always have a choice to operate from our best self or not. Knowing this has power.

First and Foremost: Notice, Notice, Notice

If I asked you to write it down I'm sure you would be able to pin point times in your life, the past week or even today where this voice in your head has been reactive, agitated, loud, angry, frustrated, distracted, worried, obsessively stuck going over conversations had in the way you wish they had been had or playing out scenarios and their imaginary outcomes ...... and times at the other end of the scale when you have felt a sense of peace where the mind is quieter, you are relaxed, happy, present, focused, confident and calm: where you work in a sense of effortless ease. This is a state of being first named by Hungarian Psychologist Mihály Csíkszentmihályi as "being in flow".

There will be a difference in how you show up in the times that your mind is activated, distracted and the times you are clear. In simple terms, one will paint a picture of you at your best the other when you are not – when what is on display is the side of yourself that you least like, that others least like, that avoids, that creates conflict, that does not tend to get you the best results, that you may go at great lengths to hide but is there none the less in all of us.

There is a brilliant book I was asked to read a good 15 years ago when I did that first Leadership Mindsets training, called *Leadership and Self-Deception* by the Arbinger Institute. (The Arbinger Institute, 2008) It is written as a fictional story through the eyes of a leader who joins a new company and is being coached by his CEO in a framework for understanding Mindset, a philosophy that sits at the heart of the organisation's success. Self-deception is described as a form of blindness to the part we are playing in keeping ourselves stuck. It is a victim state where our tendency is to try harder and harder to make things work, where we often blame everyone and everything else for why things are as they are.

A state where we in fact have the problem but we are often the last to see it.

Out of the box:
When I'm at my best, in flow

e.g. proactive, creative, clear, connected,
confident, powerful, purposeful

In the box:
When I'm not at my best

e.g. frustrated, irritable, fearful, stressed,
low in energy, flat, indecisive, powerless

The framework it uses is simple: In and Out of the
Box. *In the Box* we are quite literally limited, driven
by our beliefs, our demands of how we or others
should be and self-justifications of our own rightness.
In the Box we inflate both our own virtue and the
faults of others. *In the Box* we show up in a way that
invites others to be *In the Box*.

Out of the Box we are aware and purposeful. We
see others as they are; as people, not objects. How
we act, behave, speak to others, listen, come up
with ideas and make decisions are from our best
self. A state of mind and being that we choose.
And the thing about state is that it leads state,
which is good to know. As however we are
choosing to show up, whether it is *In or Out of the*

Box, tends to be reflected back at us by those we work and live alongside. Optimism, creativity, hope and joy breeds the same and quite effortlessly brings others up. Anger, frustration, negativity and avoidance breed the same and will drag others down. This is how engagement works. Either way, our own state is infectious, and the great news is that we have the choice as to which it is to be.

When all is going amazingly well, it is easy to see how it is possible to stay *Out of the Box*. It is only when we hit a problem, an issue or a block that we are challenged. Where the invitation to get *In the Box* presents itself and it becomes seductively easy to point the finger on what is going on outside of us. But when challenged this is the time to take a look at ourselves first. Overcoming a problem *In the Box* is rarely a great way to get the best result, even if the problem does lie elsewhere.

"When we are no longer able to change a situation, we are challenged to change ourselves."

- **Viktor Frankl**

This speaks to knowing what it is we can control. There are really only ever two options: change your circumstances or change the way you think about them.

If you or someone close to you has ever found yourself repeating a pattern: going from company to company, job to job and finding similar themes, issues, patterns of conflict and disconnect are re-occurring, then it is likely that the issues in some shape or form lie on the inside rather than the outside. As a great coach and friend of mine often says, you can think moving on is the answer, but you know you take yourself wherever you go.

The key to determining which it is requires a closer examination of the voice in your head. What I will refer to as the 'Filter'. In short: what is the voice saying? (Remembering that this voice does a great running commentary of what has happened in the past, what this means will happen in the future and what others will think of us). The question to look at when observing the running commentary in the mind is how much of any of it is actually true?

I run many workshops on subject of Feedback and one of the exercises I always do is to look at the associations we have about feedback, our own experiences that stand out as pivotal for the good and not so good, and as a result what have we come to believe, and assume about our ability to give it and receive it.

Here are some example Filters (beliefs, judgments, predictions) about giving feedback that I uncovered in a recent workshop:

- Feedback here is largely negative

- If someone says "Can I have a minute?" I think what have I done wrong?

- When I give upwards challenge and feedback I get faced with anger and hostility, I feel in the wrong and think what's the point?

- We have an awkward conversation room, if you get asked to go in there you know you are screwed

- Performance Management is time consuming and only puts a strain on the relationship

- Performance conversations are really uncomfortable for both parties, so I generally avoid them

No surprises that feedback was an issue, something that had nothing to do with calibre of the leadership team or the organisation's HR processes, and everything to do with their Mindset. There was no 'awkward conversation room' it was in fact just another office. Their actions post workshop proved quite categorically that performance management could be simple and did not have to take inordinate amounts of time. The issue was that conversations that needed to be had were not happening and this had everything to do with the running commentary of fears and beliefs in their minds. All of which were false.

The team were collectively *In the Box* in relation to feedback. Which, of course, is an issue, as any kind of dialogue, engagement or communication you want to result in someone else doing something more of, less of or differently will rarely work as long as you are *In the Box*.

Being *In the Box* is a problem which creates other serious problems. When the difficult conversations that need to be had with team members, peers and those more senior are not happening, issues persist and worsen. Momentum and progress slow down with the burden of carrying under-performance.

Engagement takes a dip. And when you start to hear the rumblings of discontent on the inside you can be sure you will eventually hear it from the outside if the issues going unaddressed mean that your customers and consumers start to disconnect.

When the pain to the organisation and team starts to outweigh the personal discomfort involved in speaking up, then you generally have a good enough reason to challenge the beliefs and predictions of the Filter.

But of course, there is also our own personal reputation. When fear is in the driving seat, we can hold back from telling the truth, can overly rely on process and changing structures which can be seen as far easier to control but don't confront the real issue. I lose count how many teams I have witnessed attempting to solve performance issues by changing organisational structures: an act of leadership avoidance that in itself creates more fear, uncertainty and opportunity for your stars to leave and be paid for the pleasure. In avoidance we stop role modelling what we know is right, like being honest with people. We also fail to act in alignment with what we may say is important. Most leaders will tell me that they welcome feedback and be able to recite the feedback which was pivotal to their own development and career. All will run performance reviews, which is usually accompanied by a lengthy form. But are all having open and honest conversations? No. Do their HRDs trust that what gets put on the forms is a true representation of their talent? Rarely. Are all leaders actually aligned on what great looks like? Not always.

This becomes an issue of integrity. Anytime we are *In the Box*; in self-deception, there is a cost to our integrity, as we are not operating from who we are at heart, when we are at our best, focusing on who and what matters most.

Getting Out of the Box

Noticing we are part of the problem is the first step: Either by feeling the cost of not being in alignment which provides a powerful energetic charge to get *Out of the Box*, or by realising that what we are individually or collectively believing is in fact false.

The way to stay *Out of the Box* as much as is humanly possible is simply to find your purpose.

Following the example I ran with this team, I asked why does feedback matter to you? And this is what they said:

- Feedback drives innovation, growth, results, and drives the organisation's success and the people in it (the bigger picture).

- Whether the purpose is to reward, grow or hold a boundary, feedback is one of those responsibilities in leadership where avoidance is not actually a viable option. It is our job. And if we want to stay here in this organisation, this is what we do (the bottom line)

- It is the day in, day out commitment to openness, honesty, support and progress (connection to values)

- Because it is a chance for each and every leader to do and say the right thing: for themselves, for others, for the organisation (personal integrity).

Tapping into our purpose drives clarity and focuses energy. It inspires us to act from our best self. With purpose, anything you say or do is much more likely to have more powerful influence on others. If the purpose is meaningful, it will be enough to outweigh the fear. Honestly, it doesn't really matter which angle you take when it comes to purpose - whether it for you, for others, for the organisation or society as a whole. What matters is that it means something to you.

I was coaching a client recently who is a director of a large organisation. One of the reasons that he wanted support was to overcome procrastination. He is an incredibly bright, exceptionally astute strategic thinker; a balanced thoughtful introvert who is an incredible communicator and influencer.

One of his strengths brings with it a downside. At his best he has an amazing ability to step back, see the big picture in all its complexity and to weigh up alternatives to find the best way forward. When not at his best, this same quality can overwhelm him. The thoughtfulness goes into overdrive and it tips into over thinking. He turns inward, and his energy slows in line with his decision-making. We did some work on 3 projects where he knew he was procrastinating. This was causing issues – both in terms of missed deadlines and where in seeking the views of others, which were all conflicting, he had lost confidence in which was "right".

Listening to the voice in his head, his Filter, showed that in all three situations he was fearful of making the wrong decision. What he realised very quickly was that his energy shifted when he got out of his head the worst that could happen, and got back in touch with the pivotal question: what actually matters? To him, to his team, to the organisation "It's so obvious Nic, and so simple, it all comes down to *Purpose*."

When you get it, you never forget it.

What is important to remember is that the clues to our Mindset (and our Filter) always show up in our behaviours and our State. Sometimes this lies in what we are *not* doing – what we avoid, sit on, dread, force ourselves to do but hate every minute of, as in the example above – and sometimes it shows up in hyper activity, in doing too much, in stress and the way we drive ourselves and others.

I had another client who was always busy. Every time I saw him, he told me everything he was doing and everything he was not with an air of exasperation and resignation. As if the confident, intelligent and extremely capable person he is could do absolutely nothing about it. He is a Chief Exec of a very large organization. A high workload goes with the territory for most but playing victim doesn't have to. A few weeks after our conversation he was in hospital suffering from a stress induced suspected heart attack. His belief that he could do nothing to say no to the demands of others, a fear of letting people down and what it might look like if he did, had quite literally stopped him in his tracks.

Whether you are in a role at the top, middle or front line of an organization, an entrepreneur running your own business or a full-time parent looking after small children, then you have probably caught yourself droning on to your friends, family or work colleagues about how busy you are – usually, if you are anything like me, when you realise that you have dropped one of the many balls you have been juggling. A call you have forgotten to make, a commitment made and not followed through, time and attention not given to those closest to you, over reliance on junk food, a good intention to go the gym/run/swim that didn't make it because you were just so busy doing other stuff. "Oh god I've just been so busy". Sigh. Excuse nailed.

Now apart from being a brilliant excuse for what we avoid or don't do, being busy can become a bit of an addiction. If you are someone who just loves getting stuff done, it brings a huge sense of achievement and pride. If you are just really good at holding a lot and getting through stuff at pace, it tends to get you promoted too. For others, who get busy doing a huge amount for other people there are undoubtedly massive rewards to be found in giving, and in being needed.

But like anything in life, let it get out of balance and the addiction to being busy can come at a cost. One client of mine had a wakeup call when he forgot his son's 3rd birthday. He had left the house early on autopilot, mind focused on all the things/meetings/emails/stuff he had to do that day and it was only a text from his wife to remind him of the party he had completely forgotten that woke him up - to who and what mattered to him most. It was not long after that he made a complete change, got a fantastic job closer to home working for a company where there was no expectation to be seen to be the last one in the office.

Sometimes though, the opportunities to wake up can be small and every day. There is a YouTube video I rediscovered recently filmed 10 years ago. It shows Joshua Bell, one of the world's top violinists playing to commuters in a Metro. It was an experiment designed by the Washington Post to test context, perception and priorities. Could genius cut through the fog of busy-ness of thousands of people in rush hour? 'No' is the answer, as just 7 people stopped to pause in 45 minutes. As the writer commented: "If we can't take the time out of our lives to stay a moment and listen to one of the best musicians on Earth play some of the best music ever written; if the surge of modern life so overpowers us that we are deaf and blind to something like that -- then what else are we missing?" (Weingarten, 2007)

He has a point.

Interestingly one of the first observed to stop and listen was a 3-year-old boy. Other children who also stopped were quickly hurried on by their parents, some of whom may well have been amongst those who paid several hundred dollars to hear Bell play at the theatre.

Now it is true that one of the beauties of being a child is that they are not required to carry all of the worries, places to go, people to see that we do: the never ending list of stuff we think is so very important. How much of it actually is, of course, is something worth discerning.

Another is that they live in the present moment almost all of the time. Their natural state of being is something we lose as the fight/flight mechanism develops in the brain (and the running commentary in our minds that comes with it). So as adults, presence in the moment is a state we are required to consciously come home to. Something which gets easier with practice and a commitment to notice. Literally pausing to take a breath really does help. Particularly when we find ourselves speeding up and blind to the beauty around us. Whether that be in ourselves, others or our surroundings.

FFS Wake up!

So if you find yourself *In the Box*, showing up to the world anything but your best self, then FFS wake up! It is time to come home, to get back into alignment with what matters. And if you are curious to pin point exactly what it is that is holding you back, then these are the 3 things to take a closer look at:

Facts: What is happening? What is the sequence of events?

Filter: What are we assuming? What is the voice of the mind predicting will happen? How are we judging others or ourselves?

State: How do we feel? How are we being?

The Facts are exactly that. Things that are said, done and observed. Something or a sequence of events happen which is always, unequivocally, true.

Our State is how we feel in that moment, sometimes difficult for us to name but always something that can be felt in the body, and always true. Feelings of fear, nervousness will often be felt in the stomach, tightness and stress will tend to show up in the neck, shoulders, back and jaw. You might feel hot or cold, feel your body speeding up or slowing down, or a heaviness in the chest. You might feel nothing at all, as in a flatness, emptiness or numbness *In the Box.*

This can be difficult concept to grasp for some people I work with who have become more accustomed to living in their head than their heart. Who as a consequence, seem almost entirely disconnected from their body. It is also important to highlight the nuances and use of language "I feel that you are" is not actually a feeling at all, it is a thought. A judgement.

So connecting to our State is about being able to connect to what is going on below the neck. The more we are able to tune into our energy and what our bodies are telling us (and telling other people), the quicker we are able to spot the wake-up calls when they come. And if in doubt ask someone else to look out for you. Others can pick up on our body language, energy and tone of voice even if we can't or think we are doing a great job of hiding it. It is the best signal of alignment, or lack of it, there is.

The Filter is the stuff that happens in our heads; our own beliefs, assumptions, judgments and predictions which when fear based tend to be grossly exaggerated statements of fact which are usually anything but fact, and not enormously helpful.

I will share a recent example from a client.

She was going for a big promotion and had an interview presentation to prepare for. She asked me for some time and support to talk through her preparation (Fact).

She told me she felt a bit nervous, her body language looked hunched when I met her. She looked and sounded flat (State).

It was immediately obvious she was *In the Box* and not the confident, highly competent person I know her to be. Whilst it is totally normal to have some nerves, I was curious to understand what was driving the flatness. So I asked her what was on her mind about the interview.

"I am worried that they have already made their mind up and that they are just going through the motions interviewing me" (Filter).

Could she know what the interviewers were thinking? No. Did it make sense that she would feel flat if this was the case? Yes. But here is the problem: she was going into a process having already written herself off. The preparation she most needed was to look at her Mindset before she could address the presentation. As human beings we are exceptionally good at picking up energy. According to behavioural scientists only 7% of our communication comes from 'what' we say. The rest comes through our body language and our tone of voice. Go into anything thinking that you have already lost and it will show, making the one thing you most feared much more likely.

So at this point she had a choice: to go or not go and to show up at her Best or not. We prepared what she wanted them to know *Out of the Box*. She wrote to me after the interview to say that whatever the result she felt that she had given it her all from her Best self. A few weeks on she got what she had dreamed of, and more.

When in alignment with who we are, results get infinitely easier to attain. When out of alignment and running on our fear, we put that at risk.

Here are some shared examples of clients of mine, when asked about their biggest fear and which, if any, were true:

- "I feared the unknown and obviously the easy choice is to stick with what you know. In reality there were moments when things were a bit daunting but nothing unsurmountable."

- "The biggest thing that held me back was worrying what others would think of me and whether I had let people down. This didn't happen at all and, if anything, rather than judging me for my decision, people were admiring of my courage to make the change"

- "My biggest fear was that my skills wouldn't be appealing to another employer - basically that another company wouldn't want me. What if any of these fears proved to be true? Absolutely none, I was offered a job at the first interview I went for and although I didn't end up taking this role, the process and affirmation really boosted my confidence. In the end I accepted a job at a totally different kind of organisation. It was a bit of a leap of faith, but it gave me everything I'd wanted."

- "My biggest fear was the impact on other team members, the additional responsibility: what if I failed and wasn't as good as I thought I was?

Would I lose a good friend and inflict her with misery? None of it proved to be true."

- "What did I fear? Everything. Leaving a secure monthly pay cheque when I had no idea what to do, I feared letting go of something I had spent so long building even though it made me miserable. But on being asked what I was passionate about I couldn't answer. I feared all of the unknowns and the fact I was completely lost and had no answers. Once I had made the leap there were plenty of difficult moments and no safety. But I felt more alive and creative than ever before and that is what always kept me going. I had a new sense of freedom in the way I could create my life to be exactly as I wished, and I was not going to give it up over the security of a paid job and constraints of someone else's structure."

These insights show fear will keep us stuck *In the Box*, in some cases for years. What 'noticing' does, is take a look at our own self-deception, our own blindness to the part we are playing in keeping ourselves stuck:

"Would others think worse of me?"

"Would I fail?",

"Will it work out?"

All very valid questions but ones that the mind, when we are *In the Box*, will quickly grab hold of and answer for us:

"Yes, people will think worse of you"

"Yes, you will fail"

and "No, it won't work out."

Whenever we hold back from doing something we know we want or is in the best interests of others and ourselves, take a good look at the filter. The only question to then ask is what, if any of it, is really true?

The trick of course is to catch the Filter in time.

"Between stimulus and response there is a space, in that space is our power to choose our response. In our response lies our growth and freedom."

- Viktor Frankl

Interestingly, after having written this chapter about the fear of failure and Mindset, I woke up the next morning with an interesting insight. Not being immune to fear myself, the thought began to creep in. "I mean what if I put a book out and people think it's really crap?" I looked on Amazon at another book on Mindset that I had on my book shelf, given to me by a client, but had never read. The feedback left by readers was dreadful; many of them criticised it for being over simplistic rubbish. Now I had never read this book myself, the cover and back copy didn't really engage me, but given this book has sold millions of copies this feedback seemed a tad harsh. Reading it made me question whether I have the resilience to take the criticism; do I dare to do this? I had a moment of teetering on the edge, wondering whether this was a really bad idea. I paused and cast out to my support network for some reassurance and guidance, which was enough to put me straight.

What they said, and I know to be true from experience, is that the process of writing is deeply personal - particularly when writing about something so close to one's heart. I am quite literally living it as I write. It has made realise how exposing this is to do.

Courage, dear heart

Putting oneself out there, to be open about how we feel, what we think, what we fear always is. It requires the willingness to be vulnerable, something that does not always come easy to me and quite possibly to you also.

What is also true about this book is that some of you will love it, some may hate it, and some of you may feel nothing for it at all.

But if it provokes reflection, an honest conversation and helps just one person change their life and work for the better then for me it will be worth putting out there. That is my purpose and is pretty much all that matters to me. So my choice is to give it my best shot.

It is time.

To trust what I know; to trust the body of work I have under my belt, to trust what I know I do for the many people I have and am supporting 121 and in teams, just in a slightly different way.

So there are a few things to note about Mindset:

1) We are never either one camp or the other all of the time. If there is one thing you can be sure of, you will experience being *In the Box* and *Out the*

Box every day. To pretend you don't or won't ever again is unrealistic and in itself a pretence - an example of self-deception.

2) Noticing is everything. Becoming more self-aware of the demands of the voice in your head and how you show up In and Out of the box, you will be able to catch it quicker, before it gets out of hand: before it costs you or those closest to you. The quicker you notice, the quicker you will get yourself out and back to your best.

3) Purpose is your way out. The purpose of being more self- aware is not about enlightenment. It is definitely not about perfection. If anything, my take on self-awareness is that it has everything to do with integrity and alignment, honesty and truthfulness. Of being who we really are. Of being grounded firmly in reality. Of listening and following the heart, being connected to what really matters rather than the unconscious, fear based, relentless drivers of our minds. Self -awareness has a very down to earth pragmatic energy that forces a choice. A choice to act that is likely to be considerably more effective if done from your Best Self.

Action Step

If you want to give this a go then take a blank sheet of paper and think of some recent examples when you know you were at your best (Out of the Box) and when you were not at your best (In the Box). Notice the difference in your state, how you show up to others and feel.

Comparing the examples at your Best will give some clues about the conditions, people, situations and Mindset that are supporting you to flourish. Getting curious about the times when you are not at your best and the differences may reveal some clues as to where change is required and where more attention is needed.

Then, if you would then like to take a closer look at your Mindset, and the times it may be out of alignment, then take a piece of paper and draw 3 lines. I usually advise clients to take it with them as they are in meetings, just doing the everyday requirements of their day job. The purpose is simply to notice so treat it as an experiment. No judging, no analysing, just notice. In the right-hand column write down how you are showing up (your State). In the left column write down the headline Facts, remembering to stick to the data. In the middle column just tune into the voice in your head (your Filter).

FACTS	FILTER	STATE
Something happens, sequence of events	What am I thinking	How I am being, what I am feeling

Facts:

Where were you? What was happening? What were you doing/not doing? Who were you with? What were you/they saying?

Filter:

What were you thinking?

What were you assuming would happen in the future? And what therefore would that mean?

State:

How were you feeling? How were you being?

So when you step back,, where is the problem?

Is it in your environment, people you surround yourselves with, the job and culture you choose to be a part of or not, the conditions that support you to be at your best more often?

Or does it point to where a pattern of thinking, beliefs and judgments that is driving a result that actually has nothing to do with anyone or anything else but you?

Remember there really are only ever 2 options: change your circumstances or change the way you think about them.

Chapter 6: The Pivot Point

"Come to the edge," he said.

"We can't, we're afraid!" they responded.

"Come to the edge," he said.

"We can't, we will fall!" they responded.

"Come to the edge," he said.

And so they came.

And he pushed them.

And they flew."

- **Guillaume Apollinaire**

There is a moment when you stand on the edge of something new. A pause where you are poised, ready, clear about what you want and why…. and then you jump - or maybe like me you are pushed. It is a moment you never forget. Something the ancient Greeks called a Kairos moment; the perfect, delicate, crucial moment; the fleeting rightness of time and place that creates the opportune atmosphere for action, words or movement.

I asked those I interviewed how they now feel having made a significant midlife change to their career. Here is a sample of what they said:

- "I'm happier, more satisfied, and more alive: I am enjoying what I do helping others. I could never go back now, it's work, but it doesn't feel like work. "

- "I'm in such a positive place I'm finding more and more positive people are coming into my life. I'm now really comfortable with who I am."

- "I have less money now, less security financially but I feel alive, creative, in charge of my own destiny. I have sleepless nights at times, but I have an inner faith that guides me. I feel more humble and proud."

- "I feel alive! I'm more comfortable with uncertainty, more resourceful, more able to take a risk. I will be doing something else in the future and I don't know what it is yet! "

- "I feel brilliant; love being in charge, in control of my own destiny....and sometimes think how am I going to make ends meet, what was I thinking?"

- "I know what my values are and why I do what I do, I take my kids to school now and I love it. I'm more hands on. I'm happy."

- "I am loving learning a new career, it is invigorating, and I am grateful to work with such a forward thinking, inclusive company."

- "I feel that each move has enriched my experience and knowledge base. I feel more confident and energised and I also know that it doesn't matter if it doesn't work out, I'll find a new job"

Energised, alive, happy – there is something about standing on the edge of something new that enlivens the spirit. That jolts us out of our comfortable existence. That brings together a heady mix of risk, mixed with joy, playfulness and innocence.

They felt more aware of who they are, more confident navigating future change, in a very solid and grounded state. Their experience mirrored my own and it is an attractive picture. But what does it take to get there? Is it really that simple?

- **What if you take a leap to follow your heart and find more challenges that you never envisaged?**

- **What if, like me and the people I interviewed for this book, you find that things didn't play out exactly as you thought they would?**

- **And what does it take to overcome them?**

I know from my own experience, and maybe from the work you did in earlier chapters when you look back you are able to pin point exactly when the pivot was. You may also find that there may be more than one of these memorable moments where you get to the edge. Where you falter only to find yourself back there on the edge once again, and again. You may be there right now.

For a while after finding myself without the job I had dreamed of and a painful personal situation to get over, I took time to step back. "Make your space beautiful", said one friend. I took her advice and it did ensure that I was kept busy whilst my mind needed more than anything to rest. I also took time to get away. I went on retreat and coached others on an advanced residential course in New Zealand. The time to think, to do what I love, and a little physical separation definitely helped. Three weeks later when I had got back to England, I had a job offer to work as a consultant for someone else. I had got to the edge and chosen safety. At this point I still didn't think I could do this on my own. It took me less than a week to realise that this was the wrong decision. For two months I kept going in a Mindset that was *In the Box*. I was worried about not working. I had always worked hard and at speed; it was engrained in me from an early age and stopping was definitely "not me".

Another, more insidious, fear though sat underneath it all, the "I have to keep money coming in, pay the mortgage, look after my girls" and this kept me hanging in and the fear of going it alone kept me from stepping out. The wake- up calls were coming thick and fast: I did not share the same beliefs or approach as my colleague.

Without an alignment at this level, the foundations for partnership were not in place and I wasn't happy. I got through to the holidays with the prospect of facing my first Xmas day and Boxing day on my own, and did what I knew would work to keep me occupied: giving my time to support a good cause and a packed agenda to keep myself busy whilst my mind ticked over what to do next. I would do anything at this time to avoid the chance to stop and think. But life does have a way of placing people and events that allow us open up, and face into whatever it is we desperately need.

A chance conversation with a great coach I had recently met spurred me to work for the homeless charity Crisis. For one week, whilst all other support services close down, the Crisis team and a willing band of volunteers come together to create an environment where guests can get essential support services if they are rough sleeping, get counselling for addictions, see doctors, dentists and hairdressers, enjoy simple pleasures that we take for granted like a hot shower, clean clothes, good freshly cooked food and the connection with others to talk, laugh, play and relax.

So I spent a week making tea, manning the shower block, cleaning up and having conversations with the guests. It is an incredible feat of organisation and purpose. I met a huge number of people with heart breaking stories of broken relationships, addiction, mental health issues and of dreams to come to the UK for work that didn't work out. What I didn't expect to find in the guests who came was so much hope, gratitude and joy. I listened to their stories and we laughed a lot, something that means so much to people who other people generally step over and don't like to look at, let alone talk to.

The experience also helped me to get real. I was helping to support people who had nothing other than what they were wearing and could carry. It made me feel an absolute idiot for worrying what would happen if I left this job. One thing is for sure, I have a very loving family and had enough options and savings to ensure that my children and I were not going to be without a home or starve. But that is the way with the voice in our heads: it does love to exaggerate, to paint the very worst possible scenario. It listens to fear and will slavishly follow it in order to keep us "safe". But safe was keeping me in a job I didn't want to be in, with someone I was not philosophically aligned with.

It was time to think again. Three months after what I thought was a huge pivot point for change, here I was: not exactly back where I started but definitely at another one. The good news is that this time I had noticed far quicker how I was feeling. The bad news is I was not at this point in alignment. And I had a suspicion that this nagging feeling was not going to go away until I did something about it; this time with a little more courage and clear alignment to what I truly wanted and who I had become.

"We can be slow to believe that, which if believed, would hurt our feelings"

- Melody Beattie

At this point what I do want to say is that there is no timeframe that is good or bad. We are all different. I have known people stand on the edge of change for years. People who come to the edge, prepare to jump and run away again, and then try to make their current situation work one more time. This is usually an act of denial. We can deny events, our own feelings, wants and needs, and we can deny those of others. Denial is simply the refusal to face reality. The reason we do it is because facing that reality might hurt and mean the loss of something or someone important to us, a relationship or indeed an identity, a part of ourselves. Loss hurts and that in itself is something we generally want to avoid. But if change is required you can be sure that events will conspire to keep you coming back to the edge.

The thing about a pivot point for change:

1) Be prepared for more than one: if you don't make the one that puts you in true alignment with who you are, its ok, you can trust that another with come until you stop and take notice. When you do there are always 2 options, to change your circumstances or change your way of thinking.

2) Whether you jump or are pushed it matters not. When change and a pivot points arrives, your only job is to figure out what you now want and why. Doing that first will ensure you don't get diverted and save you leaping into the first thing that comes along. It will also save your ego obsessing about what has already past and what other people will think. Truth is they might have a view but one that is not as important as your own.

3) When at the pivot point, this is the time to stop, think about the conditions, people and Mindset that support you to be at your very best, and those that do not. This will be an important insight and can prevent you leaving one situation only to find you

have re-created the exact same problem
somewhere else.

Action step:

If you know you have got to the edge a few times write down the precise moment that you knew something needed to change.

What were the fears that stopped you moving forward?

Now look at them closely, which, if any, proved to be actually true?

And if they aren't true, what is?

Chapter 7: So who are you?

"Tear off the mask, your face is glorious"

- **Rumi**

For many, the willingness to be seen or not be seen, to put oneself out there, is a challenge. This can show up in a variety of ways – from speaking up or out in a group, opening up to challenge and comment from others, to quite literally being seen in a photo - there are a surprising number of people who don't have one on their linked in profile or have one that is at least 10 years out of date: presenting themselves as the person they used to be rather than the reality of who they are now.

Making the most of past experiences is another big issue, how do you talk about previous jobs with pride for what they were at the time, when you may have hated being in them at the end?

Sharing the story of your career in way that has integrity means you need to see the good before you can convince anyone else.

And then, as we have been unravelling, there is the simple issue of having faith and belief in oneself. Here are a few examples of leaders who had to get to grips with this central and challenging foundation:

- "Knowing who you are can be the greatest challenge of all. The mind demons can be harsh: "you are out of your depth"; "you can't do this". The thing is we are so good at what we do, and you do have to be confident, if you don't you can't engender trust with anyone else".

- "When you are your business, it's all about you. It makes you look at yourself, your strengths and your weaknesses. I did marketing as a degree, I know brands and it comes naturally to sell myself and communicate who I am, what I do, what I am selling but it's not easy for everyone. I work with some people who find this very hard. And find it hard to do it their way, without copying someone else"

- "Finding my own way was a challenge. You can't copy someone else; you have to stop looking at what everyone else is doing. It is healthy to have an interest in the market, but you can't find your own creativity until you are free. If you are looking over your shoulder you don't get very far."

Their personal insights are hugely powerful, and what they are talking about is confidence. We know we are supposed to have it, but many of us don't really feel it in spite of what we might put out into the world. But my sense of it is that integrity, authenticity, being real and who we are is the key, from which confidence follows. As the more comfortable we are in our own skin, the more comfortable others tend to be in our presence. And this breeds confidence.

I worked with another Exec Coach a number of years ago and we were talking about the importance of integrity, and the behaviours that can unconsciously emerge when we don't feel in alignment at a very personal level. I said how important I thought it was to be able "to bring yourself to work" a quote he has often reminded me of since. And as simple as this is in concept, we have both come across many senior people who don't seem to feel that they can.

This theme came up whilst I was working with a client recently: An Exec wanting to take on a new and even bigger challenge but who, this time, wanted start as he meant to go on. He wanted to be confident and clear about what he wanted and what he brings, and far less driven by, and dependent on, the approval of those around him.

In short, he said, "I just want to be me at work... and I don't think I am."

Being ourselves, fully, is a very liberating space to operate in. One that tends to shift the Mindset from "Am I good enough for them?" to one that starts to question "Is this organisation/culture right for me?" It also tends to bring a huge upside in outputs and the pace in which they are realised. Playing it safe, after all, tends to err on the side of caution, will avoid saying what needs to be said for fear of what others will think, will hold back on presenting ideas and innovation in case they fail, will delay, defer and at times not make a decision at all for fear of getting it wrong.

Being ourselves is also a lot less tiring than putting up a front or presenting an image of how we think we need to be, what we need to say to fit in or get by.

Something that generally gets seen by others even if you think you're doing a really great job of hiding it far from view.

So, "Who are you?" is the very best question to ask.

But what if you aren't sure of the answer?

I was asked the question by a facilitator at a facilitation training last year. My answer, like everyone in the group, was defined by the roles I play in my work and, importantly for me, at home...mother, consultant, facilitator, exec coach. But it made me think. Over time these roles shift and change, some creeping upon us when we least expect it. And underneath those roles I play, who am I? What could I have said that actually says more about who I am? And who I am *now*, not who I *used* to be?

A few weeks ago, I was on another training in New Zealand, where we were asked the same question. But, in line with the traditions of our Maori hosts, we were asked to talk about the land we came from, our family lineage, and to sing a song or read a poem that represented something about who we are and where we are from. At the end of this intro we were asked to say our name, rather than as is our custom, to announce it at the start.

Interestingly many people forgot to say their name at all. As an introduction it was undeniably the most scary I have ever had to prepare for (I am no singer, so I chose to recite "If" by Rudyard Kipling) and the most powerful, joyful and interesting I have ever witnessed. I learnt more about people in that first 5 minutes than I have in any other training I think I have ever done (and I have done a great many), and it set the tone beautifully for what was to come.

By contrast, in my early thirties after coming back from my second maternity leave, I was asked in a training session to stand up in front of the group and say out loud 5 strengths starting with "I am".

I froze.

Literally.

I could not think of a single thing to say. The voice in my head then started to panic about the fact that I couldn't think. Like creeping death, the trainer was moving from person to person getting closer to me. I know I said something, but I couldn't tell you what it was. Knowing me as I was back then, I probably made a joke of it and given that I was panicking so much about what I was going to say I had little space in my head to really take in what anyone else was sharing.

What stuck with me for years was the awareness that I could rattle of a list of descriptors, but not all of them were strengths and saying them in front of others terrified me. Caught between not wanting to sound arrogant, nor disclose that, I wasn't actually sure.

What I knew was that delivering results kept getting me promoted so I just kept doing that. A formula that did work for as long as I stayed with one company, and retained a strong reputation and relationships within its walls – but one that was not going to work when I stepped outside of it.

To do this I would need to actually sell myself: which would require me to articulate clearly my credentials, skills, qualities (the what) the processes and tools I use (the how) and what impact this has (the benefits) to people that didn't know me at all. For this to happen it would help for me to become a little more self-aware – to get sharper on my formula for success, my personal brand (which is a theme we will come back to later). But before I could sell anything, I had to get it. Only then would I stand a chance of getting anyone else to.

When I set up Head and Heart Leadership I experienced what it is like to truly stop and re-evaluate some pretty important questions: who had I become, what impact had I made and to whom, what had I learnt through years of leadership practice, trial, error and development? What do I bring to organisations, teams and people that is unique?

That period of exploration and reflection at the time of transition proved the most pivotal period of my career. Stepping back to see it all with clarity, insight and non-attachment is important. It gave me the rational levers; it helped me articulate what I had done. But not the emotional that requires looking at yourself through a different lens: not the *what*, but the *why*.

"Very few people or companies can clearly articulate WHY they do WHAT they do. By WHY I mean your purpose, cause or belief - WHY does

your company exist? WHY do you get out of bed every morning? And WHY should anyone care? People don't buy WHAT you do; they buy WHY you do it."

- Simon Sinek

I loved this TED talk when I first saw it back in 2014 and as a core philosophy; I think it is spot on. As a brand manager one of the first things you learn is that people relate to brands in the same way they do people. There is of course the rational part: you want the brands you buy to do a job consistently well, but consumers will always feel something, whether than is trust, love, dislike or indifference. The job of those that create brands is to make you *want* them more, to *care* more, to *trust* them more.

The more you care, the more emotionally attached you are, the more likely you are to keep buying and the less likely you are to switch. You are also more likely to tell your friends.

Trust equals value.

When I was first promoted into Sales, I saw first-hand that the same principles of marketing to consumers applied in sales when connecting with customers. People buy from people.

Which made all that time I had spent in the previous 10 years of my career thoughtfully crafting positioning statements, personality mood boards and brand architecture models to share with sales feel a lot less meaningful as no one actually cared much about them at all.

There was, of course, always a rational part to the sale: Was the brand one that consumers desired? Was it supported? But in truth a great deal more proved to be important: could we deliver on time in full? Were our customer services contact points helpful, responsive and knowledgeable? Were we joined up and well connected as a cross functional team around the customer? Did they, as a customer, feel valued by our people and, by extension, us as a company? Did they trust us to offer them the best value for money? Did they trust us that the products and service we offered really were the best value?

What I quickly found was that the very best sales people were the ones with an attitude that was considerate of both the customer and the company: with the honesty, integrity to do what was right; who could hold a line and have the confidence to make the voice of the customer heard when it mattered. My best sales people were no push overs: they did not capitulate in negotiations; they had a passion for service, for doing what they said they would do, for making the customer more successful. They were trusted by both me and the customers they served, a fact that generally reflected in their numbers.

Trust equals value.

My work leading at senior exec level, and now as a consultant, has proved to me that the same principles apply in leadership: the most successful leaders I have worked alongside are those that inspire others to aim high, who create clarity of vision, clear expectations, and a context in which others want to step forward, give, create, and grow. These leaders do what they do consistently well, have a reputation themselves and track record of success which others aspire to, which is the rational part. They also tend to be those who care: about the people they lead and importantly those at the heart of the business: their customers and consumers. They have values that shine through in how they do what they do, and when they speak you intuitively get that they mean it. They inspire trust, high levels of engagement, empowerment and energy. This is 'heart leadership'. Where you have high levels of engagement, belief and trust on the inside you stand much greater change of creating value with customers, consumers and stakeholders on the outside.

Trust equals value.

People don't buy what you do, they buy why you do it.

- Simon Sinek

If this is indeed true, then knowing what you stand for, what you believe in, what you care about, I think is the first and most important part of answering the question of who you are.

You may well have a long list of roles, years of experience and expertise in functions, industries, operating at a certain level; of qualifications, certificates and titles. Who you were is definitely one aspect of who you are, and what has brought you to where you are now.

You may well also have done lots of self-development analytics to tell you if you are an extrovert, introvert, thinker, feeler, action oriented red doer, analytical blue reflector or yellow visionary creative communicator.

Now this is merely a personal view point, I have done many of them but dislike these types of assessments for the tendency they have to create boxes in which people feel safe, but which can limit thinking and justify behaviour:

"I'm blue therefore I am a reflector and I can't respond in the moment"

"I'm red so I need you to talk to me like this"

"I'm green so I seek consensus and calm, so I can't do conflict" etc.

If we are not careful they can become beliefs, which in turn become hard wired truths about how we relate to others. These are just preferences - they don't actually *define* you. But what you care about does: *that* is unique to you.

Tap into your values and you are more likely to operate as your *Best Self*, in a state in which your strengths are likely to shine, more of the time, with more people and in more situations. In this state you can achieve incredible things. Not to mention make you more engaging to others as you do it. Tap into your values and you will find a source of guidance in times of conflict, where there is huge temptation to be reactive, where you find yourself operating *In the Box*. At times like this it helps to remember who you are.

If identifying your values and the strengths that come from them is not something you have given much thought to then I would definitely recommend checking out the survey in the Action Step at the end of this chapter.

Both the values that filter to the top and those that sit at the bottom can be equally revealing. I did this exercise myself with a coach I trusted in the month that I created my own business proposition. The outcomes of it helped me to crystallise how I would speak about who I am and what matters to me. In all the times I have used this report, most people have looked with pride at what has come through.

"Does it feel like you?" is something I always ask, and the answer is always unequivocally, yes.

What I have seen it give people are the words they may well have simply forgotten. Particularly for those who have lost a little confidence along the way, taking the time to step back and remember who you are can be a very powerful and important exercise to do.

One generally that you don't forget.

"Who are you?" said the Caterpillar.
This was not an encouraging opening for a
conversation. Alice replied, rather shyly, "I—I hardly
know, Sir, just at present—at least I know who
I was when I got up this morning, but I think I must
have been changed several times since then."

-   Alice, Alice in Wonderland, Lewis Carroll

Another aspect of who are you is to look at who you have become.

We grow and change.

The person I am at 45 is not the same as the one I was at 25. Some qualities run deep and have remained with me, but I am a slightly different and, I would like to think, improved version. A damn sight softer, so I am told by those who have known me for several decades, which is no bad thing.

Experience, a learned propensity to reflect over time, has definitely gifted me wisdom. I am more attuned to what matters to me and what I want, rather than what others expect when it comes to my career. Maybe I am also more driven now to do work with meaning, and to think about what legacy I want to leave.

We will talk more about branding in the next chapter, but I was recommended a great book called 'Zag' (Neumeier, 2006) recently which is all about how to build brands that are truly differentiated – the proposition is, in essence, when all the world *Zigs*, how do you find your *Zag*? In it, there is an exercise in the section on what you stand for, where the reader is invited to write an obituary for their brand. Imagine in twenty-five years your brand or company has ceased to exist: What would you want your obituary to say?

It is a fabulous and thought-provoking exercise which I would definitely recommend for those of you who are leading an organisation or are responsible for running a brand. But it is also one I think works equally as well as a personal visualisation for anyone wanting to lead a change in career or ensure that you make the most of the one you have chosen.

Reflection on questions like these will, in all likelihood bring more to the surface about who and what matters to you most. It will create a picture that is very personal to you. I have been taken through this process and led it with others. It never fails to unlock the heart. It also brings us close to the reality that one day this will all be over, time will have run out and when it does, and we look back; Did we do the things that mattered? Did we make a difference to the world? Did we hold close those we loved? Did we spend our time wisely?

I hope I can say I did.

I hope you can too.

Action Step

This is an exercise I use often with Execs looking to explore how they can lead more powerfully from their strengths....and their values.... which is a mark of who we are at our best.

To help you gain some insight into your strengths and how they can support you in articulating who you are, please take the free online strengths survey on: **www.viacharacter.org**.

It takes about 30 minutes to fill out the questionnaire, but you get an immediate answer on your top 10 'signature' strengths.

Chapter 8: Who are you as seen by others?

I've learned that people will forget what you said, people will forget what you did, but people will never forget how you made them feel.

- Maya Angelou

How do others see your strengths and limits? What do they appreciate in you, do you know? Are they the same strengths and limits you see yourself? Where are you in total alignment? And in the areas where there are disconnects, why do you suppose that is?

For some of you the question of who you are as seen by others may be a blank page, for others who receive regular feedback, you may feel you have a pretty good idea and have this part nailed. Others of you still, may feel that you have a 'work you' and a 'home you' that you share: two sides of you that you keep very distinct and separate. Whichever you identify with, this chapter deals with the principle of who you are as seen by others, or Personal Branding.

Personal Branding is a concept I think carries with it a lot of associations and some misconceptions. In preparation for writing this chapter I cast out onto my Linked In and other social media networks to enquire about people's perceptions and the meanings they place on the subject of Personal Branding. I received many contributions, most centred on being you: authenticity, being true to yourself, your values, what you stand for – aspects that we have covered in the last chapter. One person talked about the fact that Personal Branding is yours to control. Talking to a client the following day, he said what it meant to him was manipulative, ego driven, not for me. In another message by someone who preferred not to write in public, I got told that it was an old cliché and was asked why I was talking about it at all. Which suggested there might be room for a dialogue on what it really means and what could be the benefit of defining it for you.

So, before we get onto what it is, it is probably worth looking at what it is *not*.

Personal Branding is not about grandiose mission statements, advertising and self-promotion, a misassociation that turns a lot of people off the concept in the first place. Perhaps a reminder of 'those' people we have all come across in corporate contexts who seem more interested in sucking up to those higher in the hierarchy, representing the work of others as their own, who are good at the political game and who seem more interested in saying the right thing rather than saying what is right or what they really think. Personal branding, if viewed through this lens and set of associations, can indeed appear contrived, ego driven, a manipulation of one's own image with the sole purpose of self-advancement. All of which for most people is a huge turn off and is a misconception important to challenge. And yet the misconception is everywhere.

By way of example, this week I was sent a newsletter from the Non-Exec Directors Forum. The email was entitled: "Want to have a strong personal brand?"

- *Wondering why you're not getting many views of your LinkedIn profile?*

- *Struggling to create a compelling and memorable summary to attract recruiters?*

- *Failing to write original, straight to the point content about your experience?*

  "With more recruiters and hiring managers sourcing talent online, it has never been more important to build and maintain a stellar LinkedIn profile. We are here to help. Take advantage of our LinkedIn Profile Writing Service to ensure you attract new opportunities and important connections. For a highly competitive rate, you will get an impactful, keyword optimised LinkedIn profile created by one of our in-house experts."

Now of course, this organisation is in the business of selling. They are highlighting an issue or gap - the ability to write succinct copy, for people wanting to find a new role who are not attracting the jobs they want. As a solution for this need, they are providing a tailored communications support designed to help you drive more Linked In views and recruiters. Presumably, this is underpinned by an insight that better copy drives more views, more views equals more awareness of who you are, which drives jobs.

So, a few assumptions and beliefs there which may or may not be true (I would start with my network rather than focus on a Linked In profile) but it is a credible proposition that supports and enhances clear communication which is generally going to help.

But it has nothing to do with building a Personal Brand.

You cannot enhance your personal brand by getting smarter at telling people what you have done or what you do.

Because Personal Branding is not about what *you* say you are, it's what others experience. So whilst almost all of the people I asked said Personal Branding is all about you, I would say it isn't.

So if it isn't this, what is it?

Insight #1

"A brand for a company is like reputation for a person. You earn reputation by doing hard things well. Your brand is formed primarily not by what your company says about itself but by what the

company does. Your brand is what people say about you when you are not in the room"

- **Jeff Bezos founder of Amazon**

Reputation is everything: something that requires alignment and integrity between what you say and what you do. This is a foundation for trust and, as we saw in the previous chapter, trust builds value.

But the most important insight is that it is not about what you say that matters in the end. What matters is what others say. And the only way to know if what you intend is how you are actually showing up in the eyes of others is to seek feedback, at all levels, from those close to you and those further away.

During the two months I spent figuring what I was going to do and how, it was the people I had around me; who I had worked with along the way, who had worked for me and those I was lucky to have as mentors and teachers who I leaned on to help me see the parts that I could not. The feedback and support I received from them was humbling and gave me exactly what I needed to fly.

If you ask for feedback it is important to be open - to the type of feedback we generally like and the kind we don't. Some of us can have a tendency to seek the positive, others only listen out for criticism. Either way, it pays to really get into detail. If you are great at something, what is it in how you do what you do that makes others think you are great, do you know? If you have a limit that you are aware of, what does it cost you as seen through the eyes of others to keep doing it? Those around us at work and home see us in all our glory, with our weaknesses, blind spots as well as our shining strengths. Having an openness to interrogate both sides of the coin is key. We of course then own what we do about that: work on them or accept them as part of ourselves. I have a belief from years I have spent co creating personal development plans that many of us would be a lot happier and more productive if we were to work on our strengths, finding work where these strengths can shine; how we could make innate and learned skills even sharper rather than where energy is often placed: on working on your weaknesses.

Having said that it is important to know what your weaknesses are. Awareness is everything and with awareness a space opens to get creative, to develop strategies or work alongside people who limit their impact. The best most of us can do though is fully accept that we are not perfect, nor is anyone else. Trying to be all things to all people is exhausting and pretty pointless endeavor. But ignoring our weaknesses or pretending they don't exist is just a form of self-deception as we saw in chapter 6 which will not enhance your reputation but undermine it.

Insight #2

A brand is a person's gut feeling about a product service or company.

- Martyn Neumeier, The Brand Gap

We all make intuitive decisions about brands and about people.

There is always a balance between the rational and emotional in this decision making. The role and balance that the head and the heart play in this for the consumer or customer will depend on them, not you. Your job is just to do what you do, and be who you are, to the very best of your ability. To be aware of your strengths, to find contexts and people where these strengths can shine. Being you fully is both an opportunity to claim your uniqueness and let others see who you are. This, you absolutely have control over. What the outside world then thinks or feels about you is out of your control.

You have influence, of course, but not control.

Be yourself, at your best.

What others then think of you is down to them.

Insight #3

A brand is a living entity and it is a product that is enriched or undermined cumulatively over time, the product of a thousand small gestures.

- Michael Eisner, Disney CEO

A brand is often made up of the little things that matter. Someone wrote to me and said: "It starts with simple rules like always call someone back, always do what you say you are going to do (sometimes saying no) answer every email and constantly keep in touch with your network and do all this consistently. "

It never ceases to amaze me how many people forget to do this, but what does it say about you if you do?

As one fellow consultant said, "I have clients drop me like a stone between jobs then are all over me when they want something. But if you value people and value treating people properly then the little things become a priority. What you also have to do is look at what it costs you *not* to do them, as not getting back to people will tend to play on your mind and in the meantime others perception of you is damaged. "

Insight #4

A brand is the set of expectations, memories, stories, and relationships that taken together account for a consumer's decision to choose one product or service over another. If the consumer whether it is a business, buyer, voter or donor does

not pay a premium, make a selection or spread the word then no brand value exists for that consumer.

- Seth Godwin

This introduces a final important principle: that a brand is made up of both past reputation, present experience and future expectation. Together these 3 strands create perceived and actual value and probably the most important selling tool there is: Referral.

Brands are at heart all about trust, and if you are trusted, the more likely others are to put their own reputations on the line and vouch for you.

So if these insights make sense to you and you are keen to explore the prospect of exploring your own personal brand then I offer a framework that was co-written and delivered alongside some colleagues of mine in Marketing many years ago in the art of building brand value. Thank you Nic Young, Laura Burgoyne and Dave Griffiths. It is amazing how some of the simple things we did back then still stand the test of time.

Building Value – The 4 As Framework

There are a few beliefs that this framework is built on:

- That a brand's equity, whether we are talking about a product, service or a person flows from its strength as seen through the hearts, minds and experience of its consumers.

- That we have influence over that experience: we control what we do, say, how we show up, but we have zero control over how others interpret that experience. When you make people feel something, it plants a memory that exists over time.

- The model builds from top to bottom at **every** stage. Those who attain level 1 and 2 status are the so-so brands, those at the top are the powerful leaders. Brand value exists when you pay attention to and have uniqueness in all 4 levers.

Level 1 Associations:

Associations are the attributes linked in the memory to the brand. What matters is the quality of the associations. How well a brand is aligned between what it says and does, and how connected these associations are in the minds of consumers.

Association is really about the awareness of how a brand taps into the senses and how it makes people feel.

With associations there has to be a common "golden thread" which weaves through all activity and communications. You can change the execution style, but you can't change the core message, otherwise you will leave consumers behind and wondering what the brand stands for.

Level 2 Awareness:

The ability of a potential buyer to recognise or recall a brand as a member of a frame of reference. Awareness is about being well known. Awareness is not just about recall, it's about the quality of that recognition. So when consumers or customers are asked to name a brand that makes or does X; 'First named' is what it implies, and 'Only named' is also what it implies and means your brand is so well connected and well known to consumers that it dusts the competition, status that is rare but well worth having.

Level 3 Advantage:

This is the consumer's perception of how you are better than expectation or alternatives. This is what creates value and relates to the adage, "You get what you pay for". Advantage is what you use to achieve differentiation.

Think about a brand you are prepared to pay more for and why? Think about when you first heard about it, when you first brought it, what your experience of using it is, what your rational reasons for buying it are, what your emotional reasons for buying it are?

This is what forms advantage.

High quality brands lead markets and leadership brings strength:

- You can charge more for things that really matter

- You will be under less price pressure

- You create brand loyalists, champions who will stick with you

Level 4 Affinity:

Or in other words, loyalty: which is about being well loved. Taken together, associations, awareness and advantage drive affinity, they add up to a "so what?"

What affinity does for you is to make your brand "a brand for me".

Affinity is where the real battle for share of wallet ends, your loyalists are dynamite, they will stick with you over time, they will buy more and more often than the rest of your consumers.

Which gives you power in 3 ways:

1) The power of infection – obsessive loyalty spreads like a wildfire. If people love you, they can't help telling anyone else who will listen.

2) The power of attraction – tremendous loyalty acts like a magical magnetic force field which also insulates from the occasional mistake.

Benjamin Franklin once said, "It takes many good deeds to build a good reputation and only one to lose it." Which can indeed be true. But can you think of an example where a brand has made a mistake but more than made up for it? People will forgive you, but it's often not just *what* you do but *how* when failure occurs.

3) Power of Trade leverage: Is your leverage so high that people will wait for you to be available? That not only gives a warm sense of assurance, it also gives you great bargaining power.

If you reread these definitions and put yourself at the centre of the enquiry, what do you see?

Associations: the qualities and attributes linked to the memory of the brand. What are you known for?

Awareness: the ability of buyers to recall a brand within a frame of reference. Are you top of mind? And with whom?

Advantage: A buyer's perception of how you are better than alternatives or expectation. How are you different?

Affinity: The power of infection, attraction and leverage. What makes you well loved, the go to, for what and for whom?

I think there are a few points here which are relevant to anyone in paid employment: whether within the context of a large organisation or running your own business.

1) Once you have clarity on your distinctiveness it provides great clarity on the value you bring to others and, importantly, a filter for what you do and don't do so as not to ever water it down.

2) Brand equity, and it doesn't matter whether we are talking about a product, service or a person, flows from its strength as seen through the hearts, mind and experience of others. Know your weaknesses, think carefully about how you want to cover them off but lead from your strengths. This is what people are buying.

3) Get clear on all of this and you have an incredibly solid base from which you can move forward. The more alignment you have between how you see yourself and how others see you creates tremendous power. A power which provides reassurance and confidence. So whichever side of the page is blank or out of alignment; whether it is how others see you or how you see yourself, then

this will give you a clue as to where the work is to be done. And if in doubt, ask.

Action Step

If there are questions you know you don't know the answer to go ask for feedback:

What do others consistently say about you? What are the words most often used to describe you?

What are the 5 qualities that others really value, the thing you bring or do that makes you unique?

Who are your champions? The people that will stand with you and for you when you need it?

What are the little things you know you drop when things get busy? How does this undermine your brand and what, if anything, do you want to do about that?

Chapter 9: Saying yes, Saying no and Letting go

"The process of clearing clutter is all about letting go. Not just letting go of belongings – that is only the end result. The most important thing is learning to let go of the fear that keeps you holding onto them after its time to move them on their way." (Beattie, 2009)

I had got as far as writing about 75% of this book back in April of this year. I tested out material from the previous chapter at a speaking engagement I did for a room full of HR Directors. The insights I presented and questions I posed them had a huge impact. At one point I could feel the room fall silent, time and energy seemed to slow, they were listening intently. When I stopped to allow them to share and reflect there was a pause, then hushed murmur, several people let out an audible deep breath. I had asked them something that many didn't know the answer to and they had that faraway look in their eyes; many lost in their own world – which actually is a truly wonderful thing to watch – as those are the moments you know as a facilitator that an insight has landed. Where you can physically see and feel people thinking in a very different way. It is like magic, as it is in those moments that the possibility for change happens. It was a magic moment for me too as I knew that what I had written and shared was capable of creating the very thing I want for others. I had created a space for them to stop and think about themselves. They had loved that session and so had I. At the end I had a number of people approach me for a follow up conversation to support their Exec and themselves. That too was a wonderful outcome and a number of those HRDs are now valued clients. I was utterly delighted.

It was also after that session that I stopped writing.

This win had also coincided with a relationship ending. My purpose for writing this book was so that it may help other people, but specifically, it had become for him. Over the past 5 years my work means that I draw people to me that want change for their organisations, teams and themselves. I help people get clear, have the conversations that matter, shift their Mindset and I love doing it more than anything I have ever done. But the truth is it is not a great pattern for me if I am doing the same thing I do at work with someone at home.

This situation really made me think:

What do I want? What do I need? What is good for me?

It made me realise that in order to get what I want: to have someone by my side to love, laugh and share life's adventures with, something would need to change. Choosing someone who I do not have to rescue, who is happy, free, clear and in a good place in their life, who is honest, kind and strong, is key. The only person who could do something about that was me. I am the one responsible for saying yes and saying no to who I share my time with and who I hold close. But if I was to practice what I preach then there is something I would need to let go of for this to happen. As whatever we say yes to, by definition means saying no to something else. Saying no is really hard - especially when it is something, or someone, we desire. But in this example, I was being challenged to let go of trying to fix someone else's issues, as well intentioned as that may have been and holding a boundary for myself. Truth is, it is as important that I write this book for me as it is anyone else. It is important that I am taken care of as it is that I take care of those around me. I was the one who needed to change.

Again.

And so did the book!

There is a school of thought that all people come into our lives to teach us something. He did, and for that I am extremely grateful. It has also meant that I am living every aspect of this book once again, and I am grateful for that too. As one great trainer, Roy Whitten, often used to say: "We cannot teach what we don't know, we cannot lead where we won't go." Lived experience, shared wisdom and the knowledge that we are all in this together and not so different underneath it all, in spite of what we generally think. This is what matters and how we learn.

And perhaps for more than once in my life I had to let go of my impatience. Some things happen in their own time.

Sometimes more time doing the groundwork, planning and preparing makes the end result that much more powerful. The book was written in a year, not the four months I had set myself when I came up with the idea on New Year's Day. And whilst you will be the judge, I am content that it is better for the six month pause in the middle.

So there are a few principles here that I think fall into the preparation phase for any change:

1) Take full responsibility for the choices we make

This is in essence the foundation of *truth telling* that we covered in earlier chapters. It is also a really healthy principle to live by – that the one thing we can control is ourselves, through the choices we make. Interestingly though, it can often take someone from the outside to bring this home.

I was co facilitating with a great trainer a year or so ago. The group had an issue with doing what they said they would do, which included being on time. Someone walked in 20 mins late to the training with a Starbucks in hand and said "Oh, sorry I'm late". "No, you're not" he said with more than a little sharpness in his voice. Which did make the guy's eyes widen slightly. Not to mention the group's.

After an elongated pause he went on: "You're not sorry, you just decided something else was more important instead." He had a point. Getting coffee was more important to him than being on time and funnily enough after that one conversation no one was late again during the training.

But it was true. Barring dramatic and unforeseen circumstances out of your control like an accident on the way to work, our behaviours in relation to time are a choice. Time is precious: yours and others. Most leadership groups will happily moan about the amount of time they spend/waste in meetings - meetings that are boring, repetitive, get dominated by the same people and always overrun. They will tell me that they don't really want to be in them, get really frustrated when other people often turn up late or send 50-page pre reads the night before expecting them to be digested and ratified. If you recognise this pattern then it is important to remember you always have a choice: to go or not to go, to be on time, to give it your best and to step forward to facilitate or feedback in order to make things better.

Quality inputs have a tendency to drive quality outputs and when we take responsibility for being present, doing what we say we will do in relation to time and preparation, saying no when we cannot, our own energy and outcomes have a tendency to lift. This in itself is a great thing, and you have the opportunity to role model and spark the same behaviour in others. Energy and behaviour are contagious. Our choice is whether we want this to be positive or negative. But saying yes to taking responsibility means saying no to our own excuses and tendency to blame other people for not doing things in the way we want. This is the downside of taking responsibility. We have to give up moaning about how rubbish things are, and how everything would be so much better if everyone else was to change when we are not prepared to. For some people that is surprisingly hard to do.

But the point is that whatever is happening (especially the stuff you say you don't want) what choices are you making that are either contributing or allowing it to continue?

2) Make a choice and be clear about what you will say no to for it to happen.

I met one of my clients for a coaching session and he looked a different man to the one I met about a year ago. Happier, relaxed, more present and as a result, quite naturally, exuded considerably more presence. He felt transformed and it showed.

So what had brought about such a shift? Well, he is still in the position of MD, the challenges of the organisation, his external stakeholders and the board around him are still the same. The one thing that has transformed everything is something in his direct control - he has mastered the art of saying no.

"My mind is not working overtime as it was, I am more able to let things be, I'm clearer on what my priorities are, what is important and what is not. I work with my PA every week to strip out what it is not important I attend so that I can focus on the ones that do matter. And I know when I communicate and lead my team now I'm doing it in a very different way. I'm saying no and they are with me more."

I honestly think it is one of the hardest things for hard working, passionate, driven people to do: saying yes is easy when you are really good at getting stuff done and you care about others. It is equally easy though to creak under the weight of all you have said yes to or spread yourself so thin that you start to become someone else - the snappy, stressed, more intolerant version of yourself you would rather not look at in the mirror. Well, that is what *I* look like; you can insert your own words to describe *you* at less than your best....

Moving forward with ease and pace is rarely just about saying yes to more stuff. It is the dedication to saying no to all of the things that currently get in the way of that happening, the nice to do's (easy), the great to do's (which is a little harder), the things that compete for who and what really matters. Put your attention on saying no and what comes is space in which you are free to think, do and give much more. With more space and freedom you set the conditions that make it more likely for you to show up as the version of you at your very best. It is a discipline built on a belief that less is more. Master this for yourself and I think you have a much greater chance at leading a team or an organisation to give its best too. It is, after all, a very challenging thing to preach about prioritisation, focus or service delivery when you are running around exhausted, stressed out, apologising for being late, running a diary back to back with no time for the people who need you. I know a lot of people who show up like this at work: I used to be one, and it doesn't look good. Doesn't feel that good either, so why do it? Well it would mean having to give up playing the martyr and victim. Because that is what taking responsibility does. It forces us to take control of the things we can control, part of which is what we say yes and no to doing.

Another really good example of this happened in a pitch and the day I walked out of one after 15 minutes, which still ranks as one of my most memorable moments of the past 5 years as a consultant.

I had been approached by an HR manager who wanted me to meet her HRD and one of the commercial Execs about some leadership development they wanted to do. She wanted me to come in and present a proposal which I don't do (difficult to present on what I would do if I have no idea what they are trying to achieve strategically and what the development needs of their leaders are) but I did agree to meet her HRD and have a conversation.

"I'm so sorry he is such a ****" said the very embarrassed HR manager as she followed me out. He was a little arrogant and condescending, but that wasn't why I left. I'd left because he was unwilling to be honest. One of the highlights of running my own business is that I get to choose my own clients, just as much as they choose me.

Trust, relationships and results matter to me, and in the context of learning and development, so does being honest about where you are and genuinely wanting to do something meaningful to move forward. He wanted to develop his leaders but would not admit that there was any issue with any of them now. In the absence of an issue to solve or a clear vision to go for there was little point me being there. Which is the feedback I gave him. As it transpired, nothing came of his pitch and no programme for their leaders was delivered by anyone. Which is the thing about purpose-less activity and people, they can suck up an awful lot of time and energy with no discernible outcome or benefit. I was lucky to have only spent 15 minutes of mine.

It is important to know we always have a choice. That the people we live, love and work alongside are those we really want to be with. Where we can choose whole heartedly to do something meaningful. Otherwise don't. Going through the motions for the money, staying for the fear of what others might think if we were to walk away or the worry that nothing else might come along is of course another choice ... just not one that tends to bring joy or facilitate anyone being at their best. Saying no is incredibly liberating at times when it comes from a place of purpose and clarity. To have the space to do meaningful work means that I must be prepared at times to walk away. If this is done with kindness and clarity then it has the potential to leave both parties with more respect for the other, not less. The email I received from the Commercial Board Member who watched the whole thing play out suggested to me that was indeed the case.

3) Be prepared to look at the sacred cows

A sacred cow is an idea, custom, or institution held to be above criticism. The things we hold onto that can never be challenged.

This is a really interesting one when looked at in the context of innovation. There is a more radical practice to stretch thinking which looks to turn assumptions, rules of engagement and ways of working completely on their head. It says what if the thing that is generally regarded to be a non-negotiable were to be challenged? What if we took every rule and did the very opposite? It is a principle, a way of thinking that drives more disruptive innovation – the stuff that changes markets, shakes up competition, creates big leaps forward and can be applied to anything: a process, a product, a service, an organisational structure or indeed a behaviour.

Any change requires us to know 2 things: what it is we want, and what we are prepared to let go of whatever it is we are clinging to. The comfort and safety blanket of what we know, the rules, structures and patterns we have built and become accustomed to, the work arounds and the excuses we give ourselves for holding onto them. Challenging ourselves on such things can turn out to be an extremely liberating experience.

A small example, but I pressed delete to finally let go of literally thousands of files that I had been keeping from my former career. Makes you realise just how much time Senior Execs spend presenting to each other and redesigning internal processes when you look back. Why I had been holding onto them is frankly a bit of a mystery. "They might come in handy one day". Only they haven't. I've moved on. Everything I need is already in me, in the rich experiences I have had since and those to come. My office is considerably less cluttered which is the rational benefit, but something shifted in my energy too.

Somewhere in the 10 bags of recycling that went out of the door also went the safety net that my former career provided. I loved the company I used to work for, I value enormously what it taught me, and I am connected to a great many people who still work there. But I am never going back to that world and I didn't really want or need all the presentations, brochures, spread sheets and emails that went with it.

So letting go starts in the mind but often ends with something tangible. Pet projects canned, a way of working dispensed with, responsibility delegated, material goods we no longer need or want disposed of. Of course, it can sometimes mean the ending of a job or an entire career, and an entirely new one beginning.

The first step to getting what you want is having the courage to get rid of what you don't.

One of my former clients, responsible for possibly the best example of letting go I've seen in a good while, let go of her house, her possessions and her job. She said no to a very comfortable life in order to create space, a little time to think, to explore the world, and spend time with those closest to her before embarking on the job of a lifetime. As you approach 40 you are supposed to be settled right? You aren't supposed to give it all up without a clue about what you are going to do next, are you?

Here is her story in her own words;

In October 2016 my mum was diagnosed with cancer, six weeks later on the 29th November 2016 she passed away. At the time I was 36 and was six months into my first Director role. I was also heavily in denial about how sick she was. I told my three direct reports at work and a handful of friends and each time I said the same thing 'she's been diagnosed with traces of cancer, some in her hips, and also her liver, but she should be ok, it's just traces, she's scared us before; she had a heart attack when she was 50 and when she was 60 and she's had a cancerous mole removed a couple of years back and she's always been ok, so I'm sure everything will be fine'. As it turned out the liver is a pretty vital organ and it wasn't fine, she wasn't ok, and she died at the age of 67. During those six weeks I had the opportunity to go and visit her. I had a couple of days leave booked as she had been due to visit me but was too unwell, but instead of going to see her, knowing I was behind on my budget submission, I cancelled my leave with some measure of relief, went into work and got on top of things. I had booked leave to go up the day she was due to leave hospital but that was the day she passed away. I try not to feel guilty about this, my mum knew she was loved and I knew she loved me, her last text to me was her own 'emoji' created by semicolons, brackets and backspaces which was blowing me a kiss (she didn't use the phone emojis after once putting the crying with laughter face after some very sad news!!!). So I don't feel guilty because I know denial took over, but I do feel sad because I missed out on seeing her one last time - a time I can never get back.

It was this moment that made me reassess my life. Don't get me wrong, up until this point I was very happy, and I had lots of amazing friends and a lovely family, but I'd always felt a bit guilty about the fact that my work was everything. It's no coincidence that when in denial I retreated into work: I had no place else to go.

I loved my job, was proud of my success, worked really hard but I already knew that I made work my priority at the expense of other things. These things included turning down time with friends to get work done on the weekend or the evening, not always being present in the moment even when I was there by constantly checking my emails, putting work before finding a partner - leaving me having never really been close to settling down or starting a family and now it was precious time with my mum.

I had a lot of time to think driving up and down the country during December and on returning to work in the New Year of 2017 I had decided on a plan. It was pretty simple... I would work for this year and then leave my job, vacate my rented house and put all my possessions in storage and, homeless and jobless would make my way to Australia and New Zealand for three months - taking total time out and being completely free of all ties when I came back! And I did this. I was persuaded to stay until the end of March 2018 but on the 16th April I flew to Melbourne and started my adventure. And I had the best time. While I was away, I felt exited, joyful, strong, and lonely at times, like I might die more than once, overawed, proud, happy and so, so lucky!

My biggest fear at the time was that I would end up choosing work again and I wouldn't do it, or I'd water it down and take the safe option of a career break. I also had other fears that I'd get bitten by a snake or eaten by a shark...it was Australia after all!!

But I kept remembering some advice my mum had given me some time ago which I found when I was reading through our texts after she passed away – "Don't ever be afraid to grab life and live it".

One of my friends kept saying I was going away to 'find myself' and it would annoy me as I wasn't lost...I just knew I needed time and distance to see 'me' from a different perspective. And being away made me realise that I put work first because I genuinely enjoy it...and that's ok, but there are other things I want as much, at times maybe more, than my career, and I realised because I didn't put as much time, effort, energy or passion into those things my success wasn't as great. I had an expectation that they would just happen somehow! As with all things in life we need a balance but also we need to expend our limited time and energy onto the things that matter most. To me, that is work, friends and family and if I'm being totally honest, I really do want to meet someone to share my life with. I like me, I like hanging out with me as I'm a hoot, so I'm ok with it being just me but I think it would be nice to have a partner and someone to share the adventures with. The clarity I got from being away was that I could continue to give all my energy to work and just hope for the best in the other areas of my life or I could try and balance things out more and spread that energy around!!

Ultimately the reality of me constantly giving work the lion's share of due care and attention had to change if I want things in my life to change. So, it's now November 2018 and I am writing this sitting on a plane, two days away from my next adventure. Getting back to the UK after Australia and New Zealand I saw an advert for a job I would never have applied for before, but which seems entirely doable now!! I have no idea what the future holds but for the next two years I have a new home! I'm very excited!!"

She was absolutely right too, she wasn't lost. Loss was a wake-up call, but it brought with it the most incredible gift: the courage to let go.

Sometimes we can't get to the point of figuring out what we want until we let go of the safety net. Sometimes we need to just stop, free fall a bit and get back to the basics of living before we can embark on even thinking about where we want to go next.

It takes courage to free-fall. To let go before we have the next thing firmly in our grasp. But freedom both opens a space to be creative and focuses the mind. And more often than not this unlocks irrepressible joy that comes from working towards what we truly want and are capable of. Quite unlike the dull ache and flatness that comes with going through the motions and playing it safe for fear that we can't do any better. Courage and joy, from this space, only good things come.

So to summarise this section on letting go:

1) Preparation for any change no matter how large or small requires us to look at what we are prepared to let go of for it to happen. That might be something we are doing, believing, the things that have defined our past or what we have held onto as a dream for the future.

2) Saying yes to anything new means saying no to something else. This is an important principle and requires us to take responsibility for the choices we make. When we choose to take responsibility we can let go of playing victim, making excuses and blaming others for what is 'not right'. Liberating,

scary and immensely powerful when it comes to taking action.

3) Letting go is about creating space for something else to follow. In a space where we are able to literally and metaphorically clear the decks we can think, work, live and create far more effectively. Letting go before we have created, secured or decided on the next thing requires courage, but it is often in that space in between, where we are at our most creative and focused. Both fantastic ingredients for anyone wanting results.

Action Step

Take an example of something where you know you have a choice to make. Perhaps where you feel some element of stress involved in juggling or where you know you struggle to say no. Decide what then, if anything, this means you want to do about it.

Saying Yes – Saying No

By saying yes to:

1.

2.

3.

I'm saying No to:

1.

2.

3.

By saying No to:

1.

2.

3.

I'm saying yes to:

1.

2.

3.

Chapter 10: Asking for Help

A child can teach an adult three things: to be happy for no reason, to always be busy with something, and to know how to demand will all their might that which they desire

- Paulo Coelho

I love the quote above as there is something childlike that we must recapture in order to keep learning and growing: the spirit of never-ending curiosity, playfulness, the willingness to ask open, innocent questions and to place our full energy in whatever it is we are engaged in. Now if you have children anything like mine however you may also know well that with this lightness of touch comes a fierce independence. "Let me do it" they would say with stubborn determination, which of course is also an essential requirement for learning and resilience. We do indeed learn best by doing, from trying stuff out, and being prepared to keep going until we get it. But sometimes to help us get where we want to go easier and quicker, it can pay to listen to experience, watch those who do it well and proactively seek out a little guidance. Sometimes those who have gone before do know a thing or two.

So this is also a really important time to talk about the willingness to ask for help. As action may require the support of others: a teacher, coach or mentor, friends, family or a group of peers to provide support, challenge, and encouragement, with whom you can bounce ideas, seek alternative perspectives, share learnings and celebrate wins. We do learn best by doing, but progress is so much quicker when we have others alongside us and we are open to help along the way.

Over the past 5 years or so I have worked with Emma Gunton who runs a Talent Management Consultancy for HR professionals. She is bright, insightful, highly commercial and the most amazing connector of people I know. Emma invited me when I first set up Head and Heart Leadership to talk to a group of her clients and we have since worked together many times facilitating networking events, running assessment centres for clients and leading a peer to peer coaching group for HR Directors, all of which have provided some interesting insights on the development needs of people who within our organisations are responsible for the development of people:

1) Those we have supported were all equally hugely supportive of developing their teams and their Execs, but generally were more focused and comfortable talking about the needs of others over their own development. But did they need it just the same as everyone else? Of course. For anyone who wants to stay a leader within their discipline, it is a necessity rather than a 'nice to do' to put oneself in a position where we can step back, reflect, learn, receive feedback and challenge, and coaching is particularly important for anyone whose role it is to lead and develop others.

2) Most focused inward on their stakeholders' needs and not outward, with many only seeing their network as something to pull on when they needed something. Whilst many said what most put them off networking is that it is seen as being too 'me focused', it was underpinned by an attitude that a network is something to take from, rather than to give to. The irony, of course, being that this is 'me focused'.

3) There were a great many excuses they gave for not nurturing their network: from "I'm too busy." (As we have already seen this is false, you have just decided to prioritise something else instead) to "I'm not very good at it" and the closely linked, "I would rather stick pins in my eyes than be asked to mingle in a group of people I don't know". So what often sat underneath was a lack of confidence and fear. Asking for the investment or time off for self-development requires a belief that it is important in the eyes of the organisation but most importantly of course, in oneself: that *you* are important. Fear, of course, will give us a million reasons not to do something even if that very thing is the best thing for us. If something is worth it, then it tends to be worth a little discomfort.

So what I learned from supporting others to build their network is that the answer, as with many things, lies in shifting our Mindset. Sometimes it does take a transition point, between endings and beginnings, to wake up to the value of having a strong network to provide support and to help you on your way. I know from personal experience that I had no idea how many people I knew until I stepped outside the safety of a large organisation and found myself on my own.

Interestingly, my network had been internally strong when I was still in the cocoon of the industry, but it has strengthened immeasurably since being outside of it. This insight in itself transformed my understanding of the value of my network of relationships, and it challenged head-on my fear of being on my own. I was not on my own at all and I will be forever grateful to those who stepped forward to give me recommendations, opened doors, referred me and encouraged me on.

Since leaving the world of drinks I have got to work alongside the Exec of Ambulance, Fire and Police Service, Medical Directors in a number of NHS Trusts, Emergency (A+E) consultants, a Politician, a couple of Hospices, Coaches who support the homeless at Crisis and Directors who are leading teams at the forefront of research and development of drugs that aim to cure HIV and Cancer.

I remember people I used to work with saying when we got a bit het up about the inconsequential, that it is not as if we were dealing with life and death. Now I work with people who do, alongside those who make chocolate, paint, bring music events to life, manufacture materials that go into F1 cars, promote football, run pubs, brew beer and facilitate the distribution of over 50% of all goods that come into Britain. There are amazing, bright, thoughtful, engaging people to be found in all walks of life and across all sectors. People are people no matter where you go. I love the opportunity to work with them all, something that has only happened because of my network.

Trust equals value. But trust is a two-way thing. One must earn it, give it and take care to maintain it. Ignore it or misuse it at your peril.

I have a great friend called Martine Davies who worked for KPMG and PWC where, for several years, she ran the Alumni Networking Program for both. She now runs her own consultancy business and advises other organisations wanting to harness the benefits of managing more proactively their strategic relationships and networks.

Why is there a market for this kind of work?

Because relationships create business value – if it didn't there would be no reason for commercial organisations to invest in them. For some the form this takes is an ongoing and regular communication, for others a series of networking events the purpose of which is to provide both a space and valuable content where both past and present employees can interact, learn, share and develop. This is the genius of the idea: how many previous employers do you have that seek to retain any kind of connection (other than send you a yearly letter about your pension)?

And yet companies that do work on the basis that good people tend to know and draw to them, good people. If you retain a positive and on-going relationship with people who know and loved being in your business, they will recommend you on, bring others to you and generally talk positively about you. If harnessed, former employees can still drive value for the organisation long after they have left. They have the potential to be great brand ambassadors, and yet most companies only focus on the ones on the inside and forget the basic principles of employer branding – that all touch points, but especially beginnings and endings, say a lot about who you are as an organisation and that brand affinity is at heart a mix of love, loyalty and trust. Loyalty will pay back for years, decades even, if nurtured, valued and not taken for granted.

So taking a more strategic and purposeful look at how you nurture relationships, which is all this is, merely seeks to build on this insight in a way that is genuinely beneficial for all parties concerned.

So what can we learn from this as individuals?

1) Well the first thing is that if you are going to develop a network of people around you, you have to want to. You have to find your purpose for creating one, and one that is genuine and meaningful to you. Whether it is to learn, share, create, support, exchange contacts and connections, or to expand, sell, raise your profile, to take time for your personal development, or seek feedback and challenge is up to you. Whether this network is within the walls of your organisation, outside of it or a mix of the two is up to you. There can be layers within this network. From a network of close

confidants; the critical friends who act as a virtual team or as a board of non-execs would, providing advice, encouragement and support, through to a wider community of associates or acquaintances; a network that you dip into now and again for inspiration, ideas and connection (as you might have on a social media platform like Linked In or an industry conference/awards event).

2) There must be mutuality. Networking and the benefits of it are that much greater if the relationship is two-way.

3) Thinking purposefully about what you can give (not just what you can take) is a mind-set. One that impacts greatly on how you are seen through the eyes of others and one that you have influence over. But as with the point about on purpose, caring about other people, giving your time and sharing your insight, ideas, knowledge has to be something you do actually care about! If you genuinely do derive pleasure from giving, it can turn all perceptions of networking on its head. Once we give anything meaning, it always does.

4) If networking does on occasion mean standing in a room full of people you don't know then think about

how you are going to present yourself. I rather detest clichéd elevator pitches yet most of us if asked what we do, will respond in largely functional ways – describing our titles that can mean very little outside of our organisations or sector specific norms. But if challenged to describe what we do in a way that our kids might understand can bring forward something a little more engaging and interesting to hear. So if you want networking to be something you love to do (or if you don't want to go overboard at this point, then something you might like rather than tolerate or avoid) then what could you say about yourself that would make others really want to talk to you? And the answer is usually to be found in giving something of our real selves. Who are we behind the title? What do we do *really*? And why should they care?

For example, I am a consultant and facilitator (functional). What I do *really* is help leaders build courage, clarity and connection, the foundations for alignment and trust. One of the things I do in practice is help people have really honest conversations about the reality of their situation and get aligned and creative about what they want to do about it. Why should anyone care? Alignment builds trust, and trust builds value. I'm not suggesting this is perfect, but you get the gist.

Emma and I did this exercise together and it changed how she too described what she does. Yes, she is a recruitment consultant (functional sector title) but what she increasingly does is help organisations to attract, build and retain their talent.

So stripped of your title what would you say you do? And what part of what you do are you actually really passionate about? Passion and simplicity are engaging. And if you want to surround yourself with more people who have it, then it pays to give it out.

Finally, there is a very important principle that applies to building rapport and trust in any context – and that is the ability to listen: fully and with presence. When we experience it, we feel seen, heard and valued. So to give our full attention to another person is a huge gift. And it doesn't matter if we know them or not. Sometimes it can be easier to listen (and for others to open up) to those we don't. If you are one of those people who can get chatting to someone on a bus or a flight and they end up telling you their life story or people have said to you on many occasions that they can say things to you that they don't tell other people, then you know what I'm talking about. It is also likely that others pick up your presence, which is a quality of being, something that others intuitively feel that makes them feel safe enough to open up.

Presence is really an openness that does not attempt to second- guess or judge what the other person is going to, or does, say.

Listening and openness, if practiced together, allows people to be more of who they really are which is where meaningful conversations and relationships have the chance to blossom. If the idea of going to a networking event and practicing your elevator pitch scares the hell out of you or you dread the perceived superficiality of it all, then go with no agenda other than a purpose to practice listening: just see what happens and who you meet. There is no better way to meet other genuine people than to be one.

Action Step 1:

On a large blank sheet of paper (when I did this I used a flip chart paper) map out your network.

1) Who are your champions? (using the list you came up with in the previous chapter about brands)

2) Now mark an arrow between you and them, making it clear if you think the relationship is one way or two way? Give and take, or one or the other?

3) Looking at your map what do you see? What do you notice about the quantity or the quality of the relationships you have? Are there any gaps? And what, if anything, do you want to do about it?

Action Step 2:

If you want to practice your networking intro or elevator pitch, think of an event you want to prepare for. Maybe one you have been avoiding, don't generally like, or you would really like to go to in the future:

1) Who are you?

2) Why are you here?

3) What do you do?

4) Why should they care?

Chapter 11: So what do you want?

"If I had an hour to solve a problem and my life depended on it, I would use the first 55 minutes to formulate the right question because as soon as I have identified the right question I can solve the problem in less than five minutes."

-Albert Einstein

So we come to the most important question of all. If there is one thing that working alongside people has taught me, it is just how many have stopped asking it. If what they wanted in the past is still what they want now? When we enquire what is burning inside us, unsaid or unacknowledged, the stars have the chance to align. And when our own energy and intention aligns, the conflicts at work and home that take, rather than give, energy are more easily overcome.

So what do you want?

Do you know? Or do you just know what you don't want?

When I start working with an Exec teams that are stuck it is a pretty common occurrence for them to only want to talk about the issues and all that they see as wrong. This is not to say they are not self-aware. I had one team recently talk extremely eloquently about transactional analysis, how their culture has a tendency to play out the roles of parent/child, how the narrative in the organisation is largely negative, how they seem to lurch reactively solving one issue to another. Get them to stop long enough to ask the question "What do you want?" - Often something I have to do repeatedly in order to get an answer - and they go quiet. Transactional analysis is a fabulous framework to name a set of behaviours and dynamics and they weren't far wrong. But at some point you have to step out of the safety of theory and intellectual understanding and into the practice of actually doing something to break free. Doing that requires putting one's whole self in the spot light, not just our heads.

The same thing happened in a recent training coaching a team in the skills to be a great coach. As with most things, you can talk around the theory as much as you like but it is not until you actually practice and make it real that the learning really comes alive.

For this group there were 2:

1) How much they avoid confronting the truth with others: a challenge they found very challenging indeed. Whilst they all agreed that getting honest feedback really helped them move forward, it was so much safer just to give positive feedback: to nurture, praise and support. Which of course is one very important part of coaching. As is providing challenge. Staying in one fixed preferred style was actually about them avoiding their own fear, and meant they were not aligned to what would benefit those they are there to serve.

2) The other was how easy it is to keep circling on the issues. To get lost in the current reality, of what holds them back, of all the reasons and excuses for not doing things. How easy and safe it is to stay in our heads focusing on the problem. And how long, if given the room, they were willing to stay there.

These are 2 questions that helped them to cut through the noise. What is the goal? What do you actually want?

Get clear on this and everything gets so easy. Truths when spoken from the heart tend to come out with clarity and simplicity. There is a resonance and energy that you can see and feel. People's eyes shine, their bodies shift, a light goes on. "I want to challenge more" for one participant became "I want to get what is in my head on the table". At which point he did, by sharing a personal example with bravery that had been occupying considerable space in his head for months but that he had not disclosed to anyone. Powerfully cathartic and through role modelling showed what coaching, and creating a safe space for honesty, could do.

We often know exactly what needs to be done and said, if only we could trust ourselves to actually say it.

So what do you want?

It is a really simple question.

But sometimes it is the simplest of questions that can be the hardest to answer. Especially when the answer you want to say; the one that comes from your heart is the one thing your head says you shouldn't, you can't, and/or that you think others would judge you for.

I would say 80% of the time people will start with "I don't know." to that question, as one of my coaching clients did. Although she did really, she just hadn't allowed herself to say it. But with a little encouragement and some direct questions she went from "I don't know." to a compelling vision and clear actions within 20 minutes.

At the end of the session she cried with relief "I feel so much lighter, like a weight has actually come off my shoulders. It is incredible. My head was full, I was going round and round, and now it's clear." And before she said all of that I could tell: her face said it all.

I have had another two clients in the last couple of weeks who did the same. They started with "I don't know." but quickly progressed to "Actually I want to work 4 days a week." One wanted to spend more time to look after herself having taken time out for to recover from illness. What she really wanted was to go to Yoga and just put a little more space in her week to do all the other things that are important to caring for her family. Another wanted to be able to do the pick-up from school 2 days a week: one of her children is now walking herself to secondary school. They grow up so quick, so being there for her little one whilst she was still at the age she needs it meant a lot.

Sometimes it really is that simple. Sometimes a shift really can be made that quick. Sometimes saying what you want out loud in front of someone else who believes in you is all that is needed.

Sometimes the energy and ideas that this sparks are so clear and feel so right that action is inevitable. One of them told me just last week that she had taken her coaching notes to an interview for a new job, and with it her list of wants. To her great surprise but not mine, they said yes to all of them. She now works flexibly, for more money and the space she has created has, in her words, allowed her to be a nicer person to be around: happier, calmer and a lot less stressed, grouchy and argumentative with her loved ones. She was hugely grateful (as is her husband) but all I had done was allow her to say what she had discounted in her own head as impossible. By saying it out loud she found the confidence to allow them the opportunity to respond to that question, and because they really wanted her, they said yes.

Once we know our value, asking for what we want does get a whole lot easier.

So what is it you really want......? And is what you say what you really mean?

I had an approach from a public sector organisation. I had been referred by a member of the Exec and recommended by a valued client.

The brief: *We would like you to help us with facilitation of a series of engagement workshops for a team of circa 100 who have just gone through consultation and a reorganisation, with new line managers, new responsibilities and a new identity.*

Awesome, I thought. Just the kind of work I love with an amazing set of people. But given that this is a public sector organisation, I asked one direct question: "Do you genuinely want me to respond to this or you have already chosen someone, and you are just using me to get your 3 quotes? My preference is that you are straight with me." "Ah well.... ahem well (cue slightly nervous laughter) ... Yes and no" was the response. "We have already had a submission, but we do want to know that we are getting value for money and the best design possible."

Now I rate the person who referred me and with their support, I asked to have a conversation with the Chief Exec: to understand their issues and wants for the culture going forward and establish what dialogue had been had with the senior leadership team to align on the questions they were seeking to ask the wider team.

They were unable to give me any time and I was asked to respond to the written brief as is.

I declined.

So what?

Well both my direct leadership and consulting experience has taught me that when it comes to culture, trust, relationship building and how work gets done in any system; that what plays out in the senior team will almost certainly play out in the teams below. Values show up in behaviours and where I add value to those I work alongside at Board level is to hold the mirror up, provide feedback, support and challenge where necessary to ensure that values aren't just something you create to put on a poster and ask others to do. Values, if you want to have them, are there to be lived, role modelled from the very top, day in day out, with all stakeholders, no matter whether they are on the inside or the outside of the organisation. Any request to do engagement work that lacks the engagement of the senior stakeholder signals a disconnect with a desire to do something meaningful or truly impactful.

My belief is that great processes, like great organisational structures, work brilliantly when purposed to drive the outcomes you want and where there is alignment to the behaviours that support you being successful. So, if you say you want to engage with people or seek alternative responses from providers then do it, *fully*. Find the time to be present, show up, and the process and the people will work to get you the very best solutions and return on your investment. If you can't or don't actually want to, then be honest. Honesty, openness, transparency is engaging. Going through the motions of a process to tick a box is not. Having a well-intentioned process that people pay lip service to and spend energy working around gets seen by all for what it is: a waste of time and energy which makes it anything but engaging for those being used to make up the numbers.

If you say you want something, mean it. Be honest about what you want. Saying you want one thing when in fact there is another intention sitting right underneath it will get seen by all for what it is: a pretence. Not a great foundation for trust or inspiring anyone into action.

That also includes being honest enough to say no to being part of a charade.

So what is it you want? ….. Making it real

The first practical step to take, when exploring what we want, is to create a vision. I first did this exercise when being coached myself at the time I started up Head and Heart Leadership. I do it still, every Jan for the year ahead and I've kept every single one.

Painting a picture of what you want can be exactly that and personally I love working with visuals, symbols. Some people are a natural, and can quite literally think and see in pictures. Others find a blank page quite daunting and detest the idea of being asked to draw what they want. But it doesn't matter how basic your stick drawings are, as it's not a test: this isn't an Art GCSE and it's not about being 'good'. Visioning is about expressing what is in your head: the thoughts, dreams, ideas and hopes, in a way that gets us out of our logical, rational brain - the one that analyses, judges and decides and into the part that is creative, expansive and free. And in spite of their protestations, I can't tell you how many of my clients have kept their scribbles, shared with their partners, kids, team and line managers; who still carry it around with them or have it pinned to fridge doors and office walls as a reminder. Going for what we want is highly likely to involve being pushed out of some kind of comfort zone. A good and extremely safe place to start as any is with a stick drawing. You never know - it might just be fun.

So a few points in summary about exploring what you want:

Courage, dear heart

1) Notice when and where you looping back into the story of the issue, of what is not right and who is to blame. Whether this is in your own head or in conversation with others, it will be a signal you are still firmly *In the Box*. Expressing what you want cuts through the story. You can be sure you have got there when you have a response that is simple and clear.

2) Be honest. Always. With yourself first and foremost. This will help you to be more honest with everyone else around you, which is one of the most important foundations of trust there is.

3) Be open to do stepping out of your comfort zone if what you want to be different in the future requires you to rise above your usual patterns. If you have been circling on an issue for a while and tend not to open easily then choose someone you trust to work alongside you. This will ensure you invite a level of challenge where you need it.

Action Step

So if you want to give this a go take a blank piece of paper and some coloured pens.

It may help to do one drawing to ease you into it of how you feel right now. No judgement at all: just express whatever it is you feel.

Take another blank sheet of paper and pick a time frame in the future: a year, maybe 3 or 5 years from now. I usually go for a year, but you pick whatever works for you.

Simply draw how you want your life/work to look like, how you want it to feel, what you want to be doing. What do you want to be different from now?

Now taking a step back, what do you see?

Chapter 12: Dear Me

"You will never be able to escape from the heart, so it is better to listen to what it has to say."

- Paulo Coehlo

So if one way is though vision (what is in the head) another way to access what you want is through the heart. The origins of 'Courage' comes from the old French word 'corage' and Latin 'Cor' meaning heart, the seat of one's inner most feelings. So if Vision is about expressing one's dreams (the what) I think of Purpose as the expression of one's heart (the why). In essence this route in is about listening to longing, to the people we hold dear which of course includes others, but also ourselves. When we are clear on our motives, values, who and what matters most, then action becomes inevitable. As my old marketing insight team used to say, a powerful insight is springy. It commands action. You want to do something with it, and what you want is usually really obvious. So our only task is to uncover what those powerful insights are, and our most important task is to do this for ourselves.

A really good example of the difference I discovered for myself was when I started open water swimming 5 years ago. I was facilitating a vision session with an Exec Team. It was January and I asked the group to share something they wanted to accomplish personally that year. The HRD shared that she was getting married and wanted to get in shape so that she would feel back to her best having just had a baby. Her husband had announced that he had very kindly entered her into the Great East ½ mile swim race to give her something to aim and train for. She wasn't sure whether to be offended or grateful which did make me laugh out loud. But she went on to share a story of the two of them training for a marathon and the feeling of crossing the line hand-in-hand, of doing something she never ever thought she would ever be capable of doing. She didn't need to say what that meant to her, it showed in her voice and on her face.

I felt utterly inspired and found myself volunteering to train alongside her and do the race together that June. When the Lake opened in April we started training. The first time in the water did scare me, and the first 100 metres taught me what fear would do to the body and the breath. But my excitement at the challenge was greater than my fear.

I trained every week, upped my distance and entered into other races in the year that followed, Loch Lomond, Windermere, Alton Water, culminating in 5.25 mile end to end of Lake Coniston. The 3rd year I booked into an open water training camp in Lanzarote with an incredible trainer (Paulo Swimlab Lanzarote). It was without doubt the hardest, most gruelling training I have ever done but that year I knocked off an hour when I did the 5.25 mile race for the second time. There is no doubt that a part of me is driven to a goal: I enjoyed the sense of achievement, the desire to push for longer races, shorter times, night swims just to make things a little more challenging. I had managed my own Mindset, sought out coaching to help me improve my technique and was putting in the hours to practice. But what I also know is that somewhere along the line desire to prove myself fell away, and something else kicked in. I had fallen in love with the feeling of being in the water. Of slowing down, of the feeling of flow I get when my breath, mind and body are in alignment, and the inexplicable energetic charge I feel through my hands and feet when this happens. I really hope I am one of the people I have swum alongside in the Lakes, who are still showing up full of life and vitality in their 80s. This year I'm not sure I will enter into any races but I will definitely be swimming in a lake somewhere with other people who feel the same as me. My next step is to book a swim holiday/weekend away to do just that.

"Speak in such a way others love to listen to you. Listen in such a way that others love to speak to you." Anon

How do you love to be spoken to? How do you love to be listened to? And what if you could apply this act of support and care to yourself?

I read a book years ago called *Dear Me*. (Galliano, Dear me A letter to my 16 year old self, 2011) It was a compilation of letters written by TV celebrities, writers, actors, musicians and performers at the request of Elton John for his AIDS foundation. Each contributor was asked to write a letter to themselves as a 16-year-old. Some of them made me laugh out loud, some made me cry. I loved it for the insight it gave into the people they are underneath their persona, celebrity status and who they used to be. I also loved it as an exercise in highlighting the things that truly matter: a powerful shortcut for our own wisdom if only we were to stop and listen to it more.

So as this book unfolded I wrote to a number of people: my family, friends, a number of clients and former members of my team who I worked alongside for many years. For those that had led themselves through huge changes personally and professionally, I asked them to answer a number of the questions I have outlined thus far. I also asked them to write a letter. If they were sat looking at their 16-year-old self, what would they most want to say?

I share with you some of their letters and my own. I hope they inspire you as they have me. And maybe at the end of this chapter you might want to write one of your own.

Dear Me,

I don't want to tell you how it plays out, you wouldn't believe me if I did. What I will say is that you will know what love is, you will work hard, learn and laugh a lot and spill a fair few tears too. All are very good for the soul. I also want you to know I am so proud of you. You will go for every dream you ever had and each time things don't turn out how you think they might, you will find a way to come out victorious. Which is what your name means: Nicola, victory for the people. Owning it fully will make you very happy indeed Love you, always.

Dear Me,

Keep your eye on your vision of how you want to feel and be in the world. Nurture your talents and value them as important gifts that are unique to you and not to neglect. They will carry you through life and grow with you.

And remember to share your gifts in service to others, as the world is a better place when we are connected and not isolated. Listen to others and appreciate we are all the same. Those that don't show kindness may never have received love. But underneath our struggles and differences we are all the same. If you feel let down or unsupported by others, take this as a moment to discover your own inner strength and know you have everything you need within you. Anger, frustration, disappointment and sadness are often unresolved feelings. Look deep and focus on your purpose. In silence and time alone lie answers. It is not possible for others to be there for you all the time. But know that you have yourself. Be kind, think and pause before you act and trust your gut instincts. If you have doubt then wait. Time is on your side, there is no rush or race to be ready for the world. Grow into the world with grace and you will receive in return what you give.

Dear Me,

Don't change a thing because you can only truly learn by experiencing. People can give you advice until the cows come home but sometimes you just have to live it, do it your way. The key is to make sure you reflect and learn from it. Be you – believe in yourself and others will notice. Confidence is everything in making people believe in you.

Dear Me,

Your Mum and Dad think you're going to be an English teacher, but they are going to get a shock…. A pleasant one though! When you feel a bit lost at University and start wondering where life is going to take you after all that study (well, some study…) just have some faith and go with your gut. You'll find the right career through allowing your personality to grow and develop – and don't think you have to do your job how all the text books tell you to do it. You can chop and change. You might start in one profession, but good leadership skills can take you to all sorts of places, so focus on that. Be the best you can be and stick with your common sense. Let your energy drive you, and don't get boxed into a corner. You might find criticism hard to take at first but remember it will help you grow and you always have something to learn from those who you respect. When you come across people you struggle to respect, then keep moving along. The frustration of staying will drive you nuts! I know you're confident, and I know you will always have an optimistic and positive outlook life- but just keep reminding yourself of that, when times get tough. Let your instincts and what you really enjoy drive you. Never be tied to something because you feel you have no other options.

Dear Me,

You have your whole life ahead of you and although that seems like forever, it will go quicker than you think so my advice to you is don't waste a minute of it!

Do what makes you happy but work hard and be kind. Strive for the things you want but don't be greedy, it won't make you content.

Spend your time with people that bring out the best in you and politely keep negative influences at arm's length. Encourage feedback from all walks of like but don't ever let someone tell you that you are not good enough. Be brave, have the courage to take risks and make mistakes and learn from those experiences. The long game is often the best one to play. You are career hungry - have goals and focus on success but don't lose sight of the important things in life - take time to relax, enjoy your family, friends and loved ones. Believe in yourself and take ownership.

Dear Me,

At times of great change in your life – positive or negative, decided by you or brought on by events out of your control – you must be true to yourself, your core principles and your values.

You may not be able to articulate them yet, but you know deep down what they are. Use them as the prism through which you make all of your decisions.

Your judgement is sound: if something doesn't feel right at its core, then it isn't right. Act on it.

Don't settle.

You will always be a 'people pleaser', that is your nature and you should be proud of it. However, it cannot be at the expense of your own dreams and needs. Find the right balance.

Be kind and be true. To yourself, of course, but also to those whose lives you have within your power to change fundamentally, for better or for worse.

Dear Me,

Be free to be yourself – not who you think others want you to be. Do what you want – not what you think others want you to do. Be kind to yourself – before you can look after others you need to look after yourself.

Remember you are special – even when you don't feel it.

Dear Me,

Ok so brilliant, well done you have worked so hard and got this far, all set to head off to University next year but here is a little piece of advice that you haven't been told up until now. You are one of the strongest and most persistent people on earth; because of this persistence you will be successful at whatever you set your mind too. Never mind what the teachers say, that only he in your year will become a lawyer, if you want to be a lawyer you go ahead and do it, it might mean another year of work and exams but set your mind to it and you will achieve it.

The next thing to remember is to be kind, every day. Be kind and generous to those around you, particularly on the days when you are having a really tough time, those are the days you need to be extra kind to others. It will feel counterintuitive and not what you want to do at the time (you want to shout and scream and snap) but before you do anything think kind, speak kind, be kind... and genuine at all times. That way all of the amazing work you do will not be undone by the big fat BUT, 'she is amazing at her work but sometimes she is a bit snappy' and so on and so forth.

The final piece of advice is to always listen to feedback, but not all of it! Sometimes you will come across people in life who for one reason or another will try to make you feel bad about yourself and sometimes these people will be your boss. They will have their own insecurities and often that will be their motivation for making you feel bad about yourself. There will be something in what they have to say so dig deep and work out what it is, maybe you are pushing them too hard and maybe you are going beyond your remit. Try your best always to work out what it is they are saying and then change your approach when working with them.

You are an amazing, person just never forget that, but prioritise you, take time for yourself, look after yourself and you can do anything you like.

Dear Me,

Things might not work out the way you think they will, but it'll be ok. Don't measure whether you're in the right place in your life by where other people are in theirs, each journey is different and you just have to trust that what's meant to happen will happen if you stay open to all possibilities.

Dear Me,

What is the rush? Stop, take a look around and be grateful for all you have and the chances you have and will be given in your life. Work hard but focus on the right stuff. Do the right thing even when it is not easy. Don't worry so much, things have a way of sorting themselves out. It's OK to make mistakes, it means you are learning, own them and grow better because of them. Not everything in life is perfect but it is perfect enough. Listen to Sunscreen and whilst you will not believe it now, you will in the future. Make the most of every day.

Dear Me,

You are thinking about where to go to college – why not take the leap? It's tempting to stay with your friends. But just imagine how many incredible adventures may lie ahead if you make that change? There was a seed of excitement wasn't there? Go! Really what is the worst that will happen? Your friends will stay true if that is how life is meant to be. You owe it to yourself, for every time you have ever doubted yourself, to open as many doors for your future self as you possibly can. You see having a choice is what makes the difference. When life throws its challenges – and it will – if you have invested in yourself your mind and body will repay you by giving a bedrock that allows you the resilience to say no and the option to choose the path that will make you the happiest. That is what it takes to change: The desire to experience change. The strength to want change and the imagination to see what change can bring.

Dear Me,

If I was going to give you any advice I would say 'live big, love openly, and don't hide'. Particularly whilst the stakes are still relatively low. There will be plenty of opportunities to explore and find out about all the things you are curious and enthusiastic about. Try to be patient and don't spread yourself too thinly. You don't have to do everything all at once. It's impossible. Oh, and the need to please everyone else all of the time. Also impossible. YOU ARE ENOUGH, JUST AS YOU ARE.

Dear Me,

There will be lots of challenges as you go through life and you will get through them all, as you are a strong, determined individual. Remember you are loved deeply and please, please, please, do not be too hard on yourself. You have a lot to offer and spending time overthinking, re-running scenarios through your head will serve no purpose whatsoever and will only make you unhappy. Put life experiences down to exactly that, experience - learn to accept it and move on. You will have a lovely family, who adore you. They will be your number one priority. Everything comes back to them. Ensure you make quality time for them, listen to them, hug them, kiss them, enjoy their company, create some wonderful memories and treasure them deeply. They are your number one fans and will be there for you no matter what. Ensure you surround yourself with as many positive people as you can, the ones who are cheering for you loudly from the sidelines. Be prepared to let the negative ones go. Lots of people will come and go in your life and the ones that matter will stay. Your friendship circle will ebb and flow over the years and as you get older, you will realise that quality beats quantity. Don't waste your precious time on those who do not make time for you. Find out who really cares about you and cherish them deeply. And lastly, don't fill your time being busy – being busy will not necessarily make you happy. You will crave some quiet time. Make that time. If you don't look after yourself who will? Create some quality time for yourself - some much-needed downtime. Meditate, keep learning new things and challenge yourself to be the best version of yourself you can be. Most of all......

be happy in whatever you do!

Dear Me,

The trick is to have the ability to turn your life style round in the short term and not have any regrets, concerns or "what ifs" as you progress through the medium and onto the long term. So always prepare, plan, think ahead and then keep on track and do not turn back. I never did do a full season of MX but then there are far more important things in life and long-term fulfilment.

Dear Me,

What a life you have ahead of you! There will be highs. There will be lows. In the quiet moments, those moments between the fun. laugher, happiness, excitement, sadness, loneliness and any other emotion you may experience, there is one truth. The whole world is ahead of you and you can choose the path you take. Anything you put your mind to is possible. Remember to trust your gut instincts and intuitions. Be strong, be brave, take chances, be open and curious to the opportunities you come across. Keep smiling and go forward with kindness, grace, gratitude and an open heart.

Dear Me,

Do what you love, what makes you happy, what gives you a buzz, what feeds you soul. You might need to try different jobs, different cultures, but once you realise the formula that works for you, do not accept second best. Work with like- minded people, in companies that promote team work, that value YOU for what YOU bring to the table. At all costs, avoid companies that take your energy, that do not encourage your ideas, that are over complicated, and ones who are driven by politics – these will hold you back & make you miserable! And lastly, believe in yourself – you are AMAZING!

Dear Me,

You are, and always will be, dyslexic. This is not a handy cap, it is a blessing! It will take you a few years to work this out, but you get it, and use it to your advantage. In the 2019 world, everyone seems to think it is important to have a label, a belonging, you have never really been one for this, not then, or now. You enjoy being you. This is something given to you by mum, your home life, and always being told to give everything a go! It is the primary reason you have, and always will, want to help others around you. Captaining a rugby team, running a business, it is all about encouraging those around you to succeed to the best of their ability.

Like yourself. This has proven to be a difficult part of your life, but now I can confirm you have achieved this in spades! You are a "weather setter". Go gentle through your twenties, don't rush in to anything, you're are a lover and enjoy being in love, watch out for "snowball relationships" which roll you up in ways that can only end in hurt. You will be told, when you need time to like yourself, as you take lifes knocks, disappointments and excitements, to get "some sand through your toes". This statement has stood you in good stead on more than one occasion. Go do it. The act of taking your shoes and socks off, standing on a beach looking out to sea and crunching up your toes is the most therapeutic thing you will find to do!

Advice. You will recognise at an early professional age that you need to go find a "silver top". This is a person older and wiser than you. They have been there, done that, and will help you find your path. You will be very lucky to find 3 mentors. Good advice is very difficult to find, a mentor you click with is even harder, but you do this well. Your first being your stepfather, who is an only child, so has no real understanding of children or young adults, but you talk to him, you listen, and you have learnt probably the most valuable professional lesson of your life – you cannot live above your means. Your second mentor will appear as you develop your business. The greatest knock, and as it worked out, your greatest opportunity, will be when your fledgling business is shattered by your business partner winding up the joint business whilst you are on holiday! Listening to the advice of this silver top was life changing! He unfortunately has since died, but I now look back and realise what he did for me. As you get stronger in business, and realise that people migrate to be with you, and want to work for you, due to your fairness, openness and understanding, you will find your third mentor; a very successful person working in an abstract industry to your own. But their advice and support becomes worth its weight in gold, literally! So that is all I can help you with. You have a good moral compass, you play with a straight bat and do not like injustice. These values will mean you will succeed in any environment. Good luck

I also sent my mum the questions. She didn't want to answer them. She said she would leave it to my dad: she thought he would say it better. I asked her anyway what wisdom she would want to share, and she said that "Many people look for answers outside of themselves, but we often know the answers ourselves if we listen". I then asked that if the 16-year-old Jen was in front of her now, what would she want to say? "I would give her a hug" she replied, "She really needed one". I don't think my mum had anything to fear at all. What she said was simple, insightful and beautifully put. And it is true, that sometimes no words are needed, one gesture of kindness really can say it all.

One thing I would say is that when I received these letters I was overwhelmed by how many people said that whilst they found it extremely hard, they found it a hugely cathartic experience and absolutely loved doing it. The letters made them think very deeply about who and what truly mattered now, and will ever matter. One person said to me "If only we asked ourselves these questions more often" and another "if only we treated ourselves with the same kindness now as we would if that 16-year-old was indeed in front of us".

I also had one response from someone who didn't feel able to able to do it. "in part why I did not respond is that I was avoiding thinking too deeply about what I did, why and how…. I am sorry for letting you down and not having the courage to confront that openly with you."

He didn't let me down at all. Far from it. He is a huge supporter of mine. It wasn't the right time that's all and one day when it is, and he has a purpose for himself, I'm sure he will put pen to paper. And he wasn't alone in not doing it. A handful of amazing clients did not do it either. Knowing them as I do it was because they worried about not getting it right and being published for all to see. I am the one writing this book so I know exactly how that feels. Now that they have seen how others responded, I am sure there will be a few that wished they had (and for the record, it is never too late to write it or send it over ☺).

But for all those who did, each and every connection I had with my clients and loved ones about their experience of doing this exercise went far beyond these letters, as what their responses gave me was hope and renewed belief. The act of asking meaningful questions and sharing learning and wisdom is incredibly powerful, engaging and drives a clarity that is laser sharp. If one person who reads this feels the same as the people who contributed to this book, then I will be very happy indeed.

So a huge thank you to the amazing people who have shared themselves so profoundly.

And as a parting thought, I was listening to a historian's view of our relationship as a species with exploration. He said something which stuck with me. *"The past does not change, it tends to be the stories we tell about it that does. What we choose to remember from history is not about the past at all, it is about the present."*

So whatever it is you write, know *that* is what you need most now.

And now that you have, what does it mean you will do now?

Action Step

1) If you would like to do the same, just imagine yourself in front of the 16-year-old you. What would you want to say? Write it down, starting with Dear Me.......

2) If you would like to share it, named or anonymous I would love to hear from you. So please feel free to post on **www.Headandheartleadership/Facebook** Or send it to me dearme@headandheartleadership.co.uk

3) Finally write down one thing as you re read your letter that you want to do. One thing, however small, that is a really obvious next step and when you will do it.

And so, in summary

"Destiny is not a matter of chance, it is a matter of choice. It is not a thing to be waited for, it is a thing to be achieved"

- **William Jennings-Bryan**

I loved this quote when I saw it recently. For me it speaks to the principle of taking ownership and responsibility. And the fine line that exists between letting things be, allowing time to see how things play out and taking the initiative to make things happen. A line I often find myself walking. It also speaks to a central theme in this book about choice. That we don't, and can't, always choose what happens to us, but that we always have a choice over how we as individuals respond to each and every challenge, or indeed, opportunity.

When we know who we are, what we want and why, ideas and action become inevitable. When the head and heart are aligned, energy shifts and momentum is created to actually do something, however small, that will propel us forward to achieve all we dream of. Alignment is at heart an expression of integrity, which shows in congruence between how we feel, what we do and what we say. Alignment creates a presence is us. A calm knowing and sense of flow that feels amazing to both possess and be around. Energy acts like a magnetic force. Both attracting people to us and cementing the bonds of trust between both parties at deeper, more intuitive levels.

Story telling (and sharing our own personal experience) has the dual benefit of being both powerfully cathartic and connecting. The act of sharing and listening brings us closer, makes us remember that we are more alike than not and importantly, opens up a possibility for the collective to benefit from learnings and wisdom shared. The willingness to be vulnerable is a must. Looking at failure and fear requires an element of courage, but only to drop the mask of perfection and denial. We have all made mistakes, we all fear something. The very best we can do is to be open about it, enlist the support of others where we need it and give things a go. Retaining the spirit of innocence, curiosity, playful creativity of a child, alongside the values, strengths and experience of who we have become.

Courage, dear heart

I have loved the opportunity for expression, creativity and team work that this book has afforded. As it concludes I feel proud of the great people I have around me whose contributions have made my work with them come to life. I feel nervous, as without doubt, nothing I have done has ever been this personal. I also feel overwhelmingly excited to see what comes in this next stage of my own career and development. I wish you all the very best with yours, and if you would like to get in touch, then I would love to hear from you.

Bibliography

Aron, A. P. (1997). The Experimental Generation of Interpersonal Closeness. *Personality and Social Psychology Bulletin.*

Beattie, M. (2009). *The Language of Letting Go: Daily Meditations on Codependency: Daily Meditations for Codependent.* (Hazelden Meditation Series) Hazelden Publishing, Simon and Schuster.

Frankl, V. (New Ed edition (6 May 2004)). *Man's search for meaning.* Rider.

Galliano, J. (2011). *Dear me: A letter to my 16 year old self, for Elton John Aids Foundation.* Simon and Schuster.

Kotter, J. (2017). *Our Iceberg is Melting.* Macmillan.

Neumeier, M. (2006). *Zag, The #1 Strategy for High Performance Brands.* Pearson Education.

Sabbage, S. (2016). *Cancer Whisperer, How to Let Cancer Heal Your Life.* Hachette UK.

Singer, M. A. (2009). *Untethered Soul.* readhowyouwant.com

Syed, M. (2016). *Black Box Thinking*. Hodder & Stoughton.

The Arbinger Institute (2008). *Leadership and Self-Deception, Getting Out of the Box.* readhowyouwant.com

Roy Whitten. wrpartnership.com

Flow Game. Toke Moeller. artofhosting.org

Weingarten, G. (2007). Pearls before Breakfast: can one of the nation's greatest musicians cut through the fog of DC hour. let's find out. *Washington Post.* Retrieved from washingtonpost.com (search "Pearls Before Breakfast")

Acknowledgements

Simon Bewick **www.bewickconsulting.com** for saying yes to editing my book. It was a great learning experience for us all.

James Crisp **www.crisp-design.co.uk** always and forever, thank you. May your year be an amazing one for stepping forward.

Tamsin Chubb **www.littlefrenchretreat.com** for being an incredible friend and opening several doors, one in April that I will be forever thankful for.

Martine Davies **www.relationshipsandnetworks.co.uk** networking genius who I met at a fitness camp, who with the other FF girls proved how meaningful connections and lasting friendships can form under pressure, and a fair bit of pain (!)

Emma Gunton **www.waddingtonbrown.co.uk** for giving me a platform when it all kicked off and being the most incredible creative partner/sounding board ever since.

Skyla Grace **www.skylagrace.com** for a chance meeting at exactly the right time, that helped bring some structure to a concept.

Atarangi Muru **www.maorihealers.com** for helping me find my tribe and my practice. I love you very much.

Mary Wride and Nic Young for unknowingly being 2 creative sparks that led to this book being born. Mary, for your house clearance and a conversation that sowed the seed. Nic for the branding quotes you shared with me. That speaking engagement was the moment that opened my eyes fully to the creative possibility.

For the teachers along the way, all those who have appeared and disappeared at exactly the right time. Martyn Cozens, Steve Ellis and Chris McDonough who gave me the roles and experience that were the making of me.

Mum, Dad, Clare for your love and encouragement even when you hadn't a clue what I was writing about. Ella, Amy and Natalie for being alongside me as I lived it every step of the way.

And to my clients, who I have loved working with these past 6 years. For all of the learning, laughter and leaps forward I've watched you make, I am incredibly proud to have worked alongside you all.

Nic Crisp

headandheartleadership.co.uk

facebook.com/headandheartleadership

instagram.com/headandheartleadership

linkedin.com/in/niccrisp

36386547R00143

Printed in Poland
by Amazon Fulfillment
Poland Sp. z o.o., Wrocław